Dedicated to: *Richard Lichtenstein (Our father)*

In Loving Memory of:

Fonda Joy Segal (Our mother)

and

Icek "Tata" Lichtenstein (Our grandfather)

Your Gifts have touched millions—thank you for our lives and for the opportunity to serve in the name of love, truth, and freedom and to help build a world that works for all.

*The intuitive mind is a sacred gift
and the rational mind is a faithful servant.
We have created a society that honors the servant and has forgotten the gift.*

—ALBERT EINSTEIN

Contents

Acknowledgments

Our gratitude goes out to:

Fonda Joy Segal, our mother, for being the vessel that provided us life, love, nurturing, and clear guidance to support us along our journey. We are honored to be your children.

Richard Lichtenstein, our father, for being the most amazing man and artist we know. You have been a constant stand for our greatness and it is because of your unconditional love and support that our Gifts have emerged. We love you deeply and thank you. We couldn't have done this without you.

Cherif Aziz for exemplifying what it means to have courage to step through one's fears and go for his dream and stand for the distinctions of husband, father, brother, son, partner, and friend. You are the force behind us. We love you.

Maya Joy Aziz for being an amazing being and the loving energetic force behind the creation of this project and the never-ending presence and reminder of why Discover the Gift matters: the children.

Peter Miller for being a constant lionlike force and believer in Discover the Gift by ensuring the people in the world have access to the possibili- ties of their own Gifts.

Sonia Powers and Rick Mars for your friendship and unyielding belief in and support of this project, our family, and the power of self-discovery.

Michael and Sydney Cresci for your friendship, partnership, and your example for the rest of the world discovering their Gifts. Thank you for being the first people, outside of our family, to financially support this project.

Dave Hagen for helping us to clearly articulate the principles and laws and for being a constant sounding board and creative force for this entire project.

Susan Newell for your never-ending dedication to this family, this proj- ect, and beyond. You are a silent force behind the curtains making sure everything is well-oiled and working.

Jessie Megali for your warm heart and endless listening abilities, your honesty and friendship, all the late nights with Maya, and all you are and are becoming.

Alex Wood for your amazing friendship and all the bricklaying you did at the beginning of this book and for supporting us constantly in nu- merous and loving ways.

Erica Martinez for believing in us and our message and helping to light the pathway.

Melissa Burns for being a rock whenever we needed one in all aspects of our project—we are grateful.

Jenna Pollock for your eternal love and belief in our family, our souls, and our potential.

Michael Bernard Beckwith for your everlasting teachings on the nature of existence and your insight that everything is a Gift.

ACKNOWLEDGMENTS

We also acknowl- edge your profound stand for global consciousness and the recognition of all beings as divine. We thank you for your courage to speak the truth and the depth of your authenticity is an inspiration to us all.

Adi Da Samraj for the giving of conscious light. You have our deep gratitude and love.

Maria Garcia Crocker for creating the pathway to many of our honored speakers and leaders and thus the road for Discover the Gift to flourish.

Richard Sarnoff for believing in us from the very beginning. Thank you.

Tina Constable for your unyielding support and leadership.

Betsy Hulsebosch for the 1,000 times you saved us (and those are just the ones we knew about). You are a gem! We are deeply grateful for you and your unwavering dedication and management of this project and this message, and us. We treasure you.

Michael Palgon for creating the structures that allowed an unprecedented motion picture, book, and online social movement to exist.

Andrea Adler for your great listening.

David Rensin for being a dream come true and a real Gift to us. Your guidance and ability to move us forward when we were stuck was instru- mental to our mission and this book. With much gratitude.

Peter Guzzardi for finding a structure we could all relate to.

Gary Jansen for your high level of compassion, clarity, communication, and belief in this book and its message.

Peter Ferentinos for being our friend, our mentor, our benefactor. Without our Poppa Pete, none of this would have happened. With much respect to a man who walks his talk and listens to his heart, we love you, we thank you.

Janet Bray and Chris Attwood for being amazing friends full of love and support and for constantly reminding us that our time is now. We love you!

Before We Begin: A Note from Shajen Joy Aziz

My brother, Demian, and I were mortal enemies.

It's not because we didn't once love each other, as siblings do; we just hadn't connected to that love for so long that it felt as if it no longer existed.

Let me be clear: This wasn't the normal brother-sister angst. Ever since we were teenagers, Demian simply couldn't find anything he liked about me: my looks, my friends, my attitude toward life—you name it. We fought and yelled at each other all the time. He was embarrassed that we were related, and he did whatever he could to not be with me. Instead, he was drawn to his friends, who always seemed more impor- tant, more special, more beautiful—more *everything* than I was.

Meanwhile, I suffered, knowing deep in my soul that I would never be good enough for him. To me—and I'm sure to Demian— our rela- tionship was like a comatose patient, in a vegetative state, near death, no possibility of survival, as good as gone.

And even if some tiny spark of life had endured, we had no idea at the time how to fan it again into a sustaining flame.

To say I was disappointed would be an understatement, but I sup- pose I shouldn't have been surprised. For so long, the family had been mired in turmoil. Early on, Demian and I were victims of sexual abuse from people outside our family. We survived, but this pain created a rift in our hearts, and the cumulative damage of anger and feelings of shame only reinforced the hopelessness of our estrangement.

When I was twelve and Demian was fourteen, in rapid succession, we lost our stepfather to drugs, alcohol, and another woman. Then our beautiful home on a Vermont hilltop burned down. And shortly after that, our beloved mother perished in a car crash.

The negative emotional and psychological repercussions were un- avoidable. Our hearts broken beyond repair, Demian became filled with cruelty and rage, and I was drowning in self-doubt and uncertainty.

Looking back, I realize that if we were older and had had more life experience, in the wake of all these events we would have realized that what felt like a really big disconnect between the two of us was actu- ally a powerful—albeit negative—connection. Had we understood more about the universe we lived in, we would have realized that no such thing as separateness existed. Our problem was that we were caught in an emo- tionally toxic feedback loop.

As they say, there's a thin line between love and hate.

———————

And yet . . . and yet, one day a few years ago, Demian called me out of the blue. I didn't know why. I didn't care why. We had rarely spoken since our mother's death—and when we did, it was painful. You couldn't put us in a room together without a fight. So why speak now? The only rea- son I took the call was fear that he might have some bad news about our remaining family.

"Is Dad okay? Is Tata okay?" I asked.

"Nobody's dead," Demian said. "Not Dad. Not Grandpa. But I want to talk to you."

"Well, I really don't want to talk to you," I snapped.

Typically, Demian, the relentless overachiever and force of nature, wouldn't back off. "I really want to talk," he insisted. "It's important. I . . ." And he began to sob. "I need to ask for your forgiveness."

My heart cracked. "Demian . . ."

"Nobody has died," Demian repeated, "but *something* has died. The anger in my soul toward you has died. I realize that all along it was really anger at myself for abandoning you as your big brother, and blaming you. I am asking for your forgiveness."

I was stunned. For a long time, everyone who I had thought was solid and real in my life kept leaving me. I lived adrift from my family and learned to create my own tribe where I felt safe and protected. And I didn't know what to do with Demian's request, because it was, frankly, the last thing I'd ever expected to hear him say. I couldn't imagine what had happened in Demian's life to cause this unbelievable transformation. Yet I could hear something truly different in his voice.

I had a thousand questions, but before I could ask one, a profound truth hit me: all I'd ever really wanted—no matter how deeply buried—was to regain my family. I wanted to say yes to his request. I had to say yes. And when I opened myself to that possibility, I instantly understood how much I needed what he was offering.

"Yes. Yes. Of course. I forgive you, Demian. I love you."

"I love you, too," he said. *"And I'm really, really sorry for everything."* Then Demian made me a promise. "From today forth, I will never, ever raise my voice to you again. From now until the day I die, when you want to know what that bright light is on your shoulder, it's your brother, baby, and I've got your back."

My eyes welled up and we cried together for a long time. I just wanted to travel through the phone line with my words and tears and be close to my brother—this *new* person—and to embrace this moment of forgive- ness and this miraculous opportunity to move forward.

"Let's be a family again," Demian said, as if he could read my mind. "I want to be connected."

"Yes, me too," I said. "I've been waiting for this. I'm so excited." This was the happiest day of my life.

Life has not always been easy for Demian and me, but it was while living through and then emerging from our darkest hours—and through the process that followed—that we discovered our greatest Gifts. Together we decided to devote ourselves to sharing what we learned during that time (and continue to learn). *Discover the Gift* is the result of several years of hard work born out of Demian's and my desire to spread the word about what had helped him discover a way to create a huge vibrational shift in the energy between us, and what I had to do to respond.

The result is the story of this book.

In short, Demian had begun to discover his Gift. In turn, his Gift allowed me to discover a new depth in myself, and with that discovery even more miraculous Gifts arrived. We had gone through an incredible ordeal that shook our relationship to its core. But now we entered into a new journey, one that ultimately would reunite us with our faith, and from that place of light and inspiration a brand-new life was about to begin. A world filled with Gifts that were there all along, awaiting our discovery.

What Is the Gift?

There are so many ways to talk about the Gift. Every day I find a new way to think about the Gift and to express the Gift. Life is the Gift. Consciousness is the Gift. The people in your life are Gifts. It is all the Gift. Every circumstance that you experience is a Gift, both the good ones and those in which you think, "How can I ever get over this? How can I ever get through this?" They're all a Gift because they're available for us to take the opportunity to learn from them, to grow from them, to transform, to be aware of our surroundings and how we affect everyone and everything in our world.

— SONIA POWERS

Everyone has a Gift to give. It's the essence of who they are.

—JACK CANFIELD

Throughout this book it is our intention to illuminate a fundamental truth that so often goes unexplored: *We each possess a unique Gift, a purpose in life that always seeks to express itself.* By uncovering, studying, nurturing, and allowing the miracle of our Gifts to flourish, we have discovered how we can experience joy, power, fulfillment, freedom, and uncondi- tional love.

We know that you can, too.

This may sound like an extravagant promise, but we have seen the power of this discovery in our own lives and in the lives of countless oth- ers. This is what we hope to show you, not by introducing you to some exotic practice, telling you to believe in a supreme being, or asking you to simply repeat a magic phrase.

None of that is necessary.

In fact, you will be astonished at how simple it is to find the path that will lead you to your true self, the place where your true Gift dwells.

Whether or not you know it, you already have the Gift. You don't have to search for it outside of yourself. It has been with you and within you for your entire life, just as it has been a part of every person on the planet since before the dawn of recorded history.

And yet even though the Gift is something we all share, your Gift is also completely and exclusively specific to you.

The Gift can be described in many ways: It's your true nature, your purpose and reason for being, your authentic self in harmony with the universe, your passion, your highest vibration, your calling, the joy and love you share with the world. What we mean by the Gift is finding, identifying, and realizing the authentic you and then giving that Gift to others. To live your life from that space, to discover your Gift, you must journey into the depths of who you are: the unique and divine essence incarnated on this planet as *you*. In fact, long before you picked up this book, you were on that journey. Even though you may not have been consciously aware of it, you have been diligently working to live your Gift. You can't help yourself.

It is why you are here.

Discover the Gift is a journey of self-understanding and self-appreciation of that divine essence. So here is the "secret" before we even begin:

You are the Gift. The Gift *is you*.

Congratulations.

A great deal of attention in recent years has been focused on the law of attraction. We believe it is also vital to recognize that there are other equally important laws for personal growth that govern or affect our existence—and, unfortunately in the past, have often been ignored. It is our intention to show that all these universal principles need to work together for a life of harmony and balance.

When we recognize the combination of forces at work in our lives, we can better connect with the unified field of consciousness that under- lies everything, in a process we call the infinity feedback loop of creation. Much like the workings of what Eastern spiritual practices call karma, what you put into the world is what you will in turn receive from it. Or, as the Beatles sang, "The love you take is equal to the love you make." This truth has been said in many ways throughout history.

Our goal with *Discover the Gift* is to take you step by step through this journey of discovery, showing you how your mind, emotions, and con- ditioning can sometimes slow down your spiritual growth, and what you can do to reverse the process. In the pages that follow, we will explain more fully what we mean by your unique Gift, as well as how to discover it and why it is so important to share your Gift with others. We will also talk about the relationship between energy and adversity and why they are so important in this process of discovering your Gift.

Now maybe you're wondering why you had to buy a book to discover that you have a Gift that you're already longing to share with the world. Perhaps it concerns you to read that you have a Gift when you believe from clear evidence that your life is not working out the way you imag- ined it should. Possibly you think that when the blessings of universal generosity were distributed, you somehow missed out. Maybe you have questions like "If I discover my Gift, is my life forever changed? How will discovering my Gift affect the people in my life? Will my Gift bring me wealth? Security? Love? Do I only have one Gift? What if I get sick of my Gift? What if my Gift gets sick of me?" Or just maybe you are stuck in a life that used to feel like your Gift but doesn't any longer.

The journey in *Discover the Gift* will allow you to understand that you already have all you need, and that you can use what you have to manifest the fullness of your life. Our culture tends to focus on what people do wrong. We want to focus on what you do right. We want to support the talents that have been yearning to emerge from within you.

No matter what anyone may have told you about yourself, about what life is or means, no matter what you may have endured thus far, no matter how removed from love you may feel at this moment, the Gift that you are—the special, never-to-be-repeated walking miracle—is patiently waiting to be discovered and unfolded.

The Gift is not something that magically appears. It is not about wishful thinking. Instead, it originates both in our passion and our pain, in victory and adversity. Some people have already found their Gifts. Others have moved beyond merely finding it and are now living it, affect- ing huge changes on our society and our planet. There are those who have spent their entire lives knowing their Gifts and walking that walk. But all of these people will tell you: to stay on that path takes effort and disci- pline. It requires a commitment to follow your heart. Not just listening to it. Not simply hearing it. But actually going wherever your heart leads you and doing the work to bring your Gift to life. We are all capable of expressing many Gifts, and as author Janet Bray Attwood shares, "What you love are the bread crumbs that lead you to your passions."

At this point, we just want you to understand that living your Gift is just that: living it. So we ask that you allow yourself to accept the pos- sibility that you are the Gift. That's all. Just stay with that idea. Yes, you might find yourself enthusiastically thinking ahead to the specifics of your Gift; perhaps you already have a sense of them, or maybe you don't. But we don't want you to focus on that just now. For the moment, just give yourself time to appreciate that you are unique, that you are meant to love and to be loved, and that you are something special that wants to give back to the universe.

Also, it's worth taking a moment to remember that:

- You are not defined by how others see you.
- You should not lose yourself in a lifelong succession of roles and responsibilities: daughter, son, woman, man, wife, husband, father, mother, friend, enemy, citizen, for- eigner, partner, loner, follower, leader.

- You are not your job.
- You are not the things you own.
- You are not a profile, a play list, a contact, or a tweet.

Many of these roles and activities are, and could be, wonderful parts of your life. But as so easily happens, you can become lost in these shift- ing identities and lose sight of how you can make the best contribution to our world. That understanding is important because, as you will real- ize, your Gift is not only for you, but for the whole world. Your contri- bution to others is revealed in *living* your Gift. Living your Gift not only makes you happy, it also brings you into harmony with everything and everyone else. Living your Gift provides a sense of contentment and be- longing and at the same time magnifies the Gifts of others.

No one needs to sacrifice for you to thrive.

If you discover and share who you are, you automatically inspire oth- ers to do the same, setting a transformational cycle into motion (remem- ber when we mentioned the infinity feedback loop of creation? It's going to come up again, and again, and again). In this way, everyone becomes an active player in the planetary shift in consciousness and in the cre- ation of a compassionate world. By discovering and sharing our Gift, we cocreate our own world and our own destiny. When we are bonded to our Gift, then the fundamental truths of the universe become apparent. Once you fully connect with your rich combination of loves, talents, strengths, and experience— including circumstances that may have been painful for you—you will find your most complete happiness.

We all have talents that we might call our "core genius" or unique abilities. We believe that each of us has the responsibility to develop those Gifts and to express them fully into the world.

> *If we don't give the Gift, we are killing ourselves. We are atrophying our heart and our soul and living life on a survival level, which has a tremendous amount of anxiety and fear attached. Fear-based living leads to terrible decisions, destruction, hurt, anger. Long-lasting happiness can only come when we are sharing our Gift. Practically speaking, we have to wake up every single day asking, "What's trying to emerge in me today? What Gift is trying to activate itself in me today? What power is trying to become itself in me today?" If the question is sincere enough, and the love is real enough, the universe will reveal its secrets.*

> —*MICHAEL BERNARD BECKWITH*

> *If you're holding back the Gift, then what you're asking is for other people in the world to hold back their Gifts from you. The more you give your Gift, the more you participate and make a difference in the world, the more the world will make a difference for you.*

> —*SONIA POWERS*

Just a few words about how *Discover the Gift* is laid out: This book is di- vided into two sections. In Part One, we—Shajen and Demian—share our journey from trauma to triumph, from a dark past to the light-filled present moment, in which we are finally able to live our Gifts. Our wish in sharing our story is that you may begin the work of discovering your Gift with the example of where we came from in mind. We want to help you arrive at a place of deep reverence, with an open heart and the motivation to go fully within your own journey so that you, too, may discover your Gift.

In Part Two of this book, we distill for you the lessons we've learned over the years and guide you through the practical aspects of your jour- ney. Discover the Gift, in all its incarnations—the book, the movie, the social movement—is designed to lead you to your Gift on a path based on eight universal spiritual principles that we came to understand as we took our own journeys. We regard these principles as foundational steps and essential to the process of discovering the Gift. These ideas have al- ways existed, whether or not anyone is fully aware of their existence and how to utilize them. Think of it this way: Albert Einstein did not create relativity. It has always existed. But Einstein intuited relativity, and after much work and dedication he was able to describe it mathematically and to put the concept into words.

The more you understand how these eight principles, which in this book we call the eight steps, work for you, the easier it is to access your Gifts and to find a world filled with possibilities, a world that is receptive to you and conducive to your dreams.

Discovering our own Gifts fueled our desire to reach out and share what we have learned. Our intent is to provide an opening for others to heal and to continue to evolve by finding their Gifts. We don't pretend to be spiritual masters or to have some exclusive insight on existence. What we do have is a distinct relationship to the Gift itself and an ability to see the Gift in all things past, current, and yet to be.

And we know that you have this ability, too.

Along the way, you will receive both practical direction and support from a wide range of people who live their Gifts and who have made it their purpose to help you do the same with your Gift. Among them are His Holiness the Dalai Lama; His Holiness Sri Sri Ravi Shankar; Jack Canfield and Mark Victor Hansen of the *Chicken Soup for the Soul* series; and Michael Bernard Beckwith, one of the featured teachers in the film and bestselling book *The Secret* and also the author of *Spiritual Liberation*. Other inspirational speakers and educators, such as Janet Bray Attwood, John Castagnini, Dr. Barbara De Angelis, Stewart Emery, Bill Harris, Cheryl Hunter, Mary Manin Morrissey, Sue Morter, Niurka, Sonia Powers, Terry Tillman, and David "Avocado" Wolfe, are part of an amazing cast of accomplished spiritual teachers who have contrib- uted their experience and wisdom to this book (to read more about our contributors, please refer to "Contributor Biographies" at the end of the book).

They will speak to you directly, in their own voices—as will we—in the "Transformational Wisdom" and "Personal Practices" sections in each of the Part Two chapters. We hope these two very personal sections will help you to see new possibilities in your life, to step through your fear, and to create forward momentum as you inch closer and closer to the Gift within.

Moreover, each chapter contains a section called "Growth Oppor- tunities," in which we offer simple and practical advice and practices to help support your overall progression. This section also includes journaling exercises, so we encourage you to get a journal or create one of your own that you can use to record your thoughts and chronicle the history of the voyage to your destiny.

Please be aware that although we often use the word "spiritual" through- out the book, *Discover the Gift* does not ground its framework in any particular religion or dogma. It is an aggregation and expression of truths inherent in all the world's great teachings—wisdom passed down throughout the ages, from the ancient Sumerian creation texts to the Vedic texts of India, to the insights of Kabbalah, Christianity, and Islam. These great truths are part of the world's religions, myths, folklore, and legends and are also endemic to remotely situated ancient tribes that have never heard of Buddha, Christ, or Muhammad.

These pages reveal that there are Gifts available in all circumstances— if we look for them. They simply await our discovery. At the same time, this book illuminates that place inside each of us where an extraordinary Gift waits for its expression. By discovering and sharing our Gift, we become the creators of our own world and our own destiny. Of course, obstacles, challenges, and fears show up whenever we are learning and creating. This is part of the great cycle of being, and is as it should be and always has been. We are here to share with you that even when there are detours or roadblocks in our lives, the process of learning about yourself gives you the freedom to embrace love along the way. As stu- dents, our work is to be open and flexible to that which is emerging and available for us. As teachers and facilitators, we must ensure that we create an environment in which all feel welcome and safe to dive into themselves.

We trust that you will find all that and much more in these pages. We realize that by offering you the lessons we have thus far learned, we benefit as well, because this process enables us to live faithfully and joyfully, according to our own unique Gifts.

We are excited and deeply humbled to share *Discover the Gift* with the world.

Thank you.
Shajen and Demian

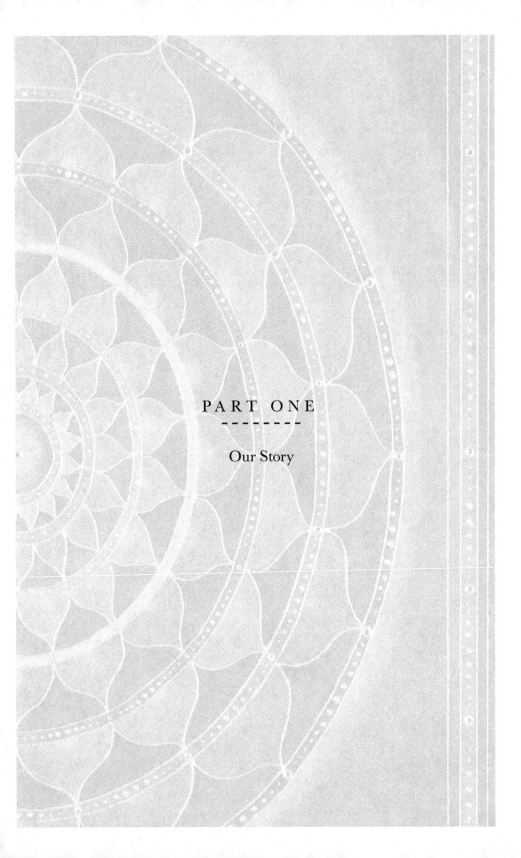

PART ONE

Our Story

THE GIFT OF OUR LIVES

. . .

Our grandfather Icek—though I called him Tata, a term of endearment in Polish—had recently undergone triple-bypass heart surgery. He was eighty-four years old, and the operation hadn't gone well.

When I walked into his hospital room, he smiled weakly at me in a way that made me instantly understand that this extraordinary man would never leave that room.

"Look," I said, "I know you're dying." He nodded, unafraid.

"What's the one thing you want me to know, that matters most, that you want me to tell my grandchildren?" I asked.

"I'll tell you a story, Demian," he said. I pulled up a chair as he continued. "Back in World War II, I was a young soldier in Poland, and your grandmother Dora— whom you never met—was pregnant with your father. We were on a train trying to escape when the Nazis stopped it in order to round up the Jews. We managed to slip away and found ourselves walking in the snow, trying to get to a field hospital. We did, and that's where your father was born.

"Unfortunately, we couldn't stay because the Nazis were coming. So I took your grandmother, wrapped your father in a rug, stole a jeep and a sack of food, and drove as far as I could before the jeep ran out of gas. Your grandmother and I walked again in the snow until the food was gone. Then there came a time when we couldn't walk anymore, not one more step, and I'll never forget—we were in a snowstorm, I was carrying Dora on my back and your father in my arms—and I thought that maybe if I just rested for a little while I could get up and go again.

"But the truth is that we had passed one person after another on the road who had thought the same thing. They'd stopped and died in their place in the freezing snow. I looked into the eyes of my infant son, who, as if our predicament wasn't horrible enough, was dying of pneumonia, and I said to him, 'One day your son will know no war. But today we have to do our part. You have to live through the night, and I will keep going because I know that if I stop, I will die and my son won't live.'"

Tata looked up at me and said, "And you wouldn't exist.

"We made it to a Russian hospital, but the administrator told me that I needed to throw your father in the trash because they were not going to save a dying Jewish baby. I begged, but they wouldn't help. I didn't know what to do. Your father needed medicine.

And I was not willing to tell your grandmother, who was also sick, that our son had to die.

"Finally I sat on a bench, holding your father, and looked up to see a nurse staring at me. She handed me a crumpled piece of paper; it was a note with an address on it. She told me to meet

2

her there that night and she would take the baby. I was afraid, but what else could I do?

"When I got to the address, the nurse took your father and told me to return in a week. She said, 'If he is alive, I will return him to you. If not, I will bury him.' So I did. I gave your father to a total stranger, wished them well, and left.

"A week later, I returned and was amazed to find her holding a happy, healthy, beautiful baby boy. The nurse had healed him. Through my tears I thanked her and asked her why she had done this. 'Because when your son looked at me, his eyes told me he had to survive.'"

I had tears in my eyes. "And so the one thing that I am most proud of," Tata continued, "is that I kept my promise that night to your father—and here you are, and who you are to me is my heart."

I left my grandfather that night, and I never saw him alive again. But what he said will always stay with me. So many people all over the world have made so many sacrifices, have literally given their lives so that their families could endure and have the opportunity to discover the Gifts within themselves and to experience the richness of life.

That's what matters. That's what matters.

—DEMIAN

Much as in the traditions of the Native American and Chinese cultures, among others, Demian and I have a deep reverence and respect and love for our grandmothers and grandfathers. We owe our lives to the multiple gifts of our grandparents' bravery and intelligence, and their unwavering beliefs and commitment to a better future. We are grateful for every life experience they made possible.

Demian and I, as well as all the people of the world, stand on the shoulders of thousands of human beings who came before us, whom we will never know and who have allowed us to live in a world of compassion for the present and the future. We are resilient, and those who know us, unstoppable.

We don't subscribe to any religious system, nor do we believe that any one religion or belief is right or wrong. Rather, we stand united with compassion and respect and love for the earth and all of her inhabitants.

—SHAJEN

IN THE BEGINNING

•   •   •

As we begin our journey together, we would like to share with you a story of a brother and sister whose world was turned upside down.

SHAJEN: Our parents, Richard and Fonda, both artists, met in New York City late in the summer of 1962. Richard was a student at the School of Visual Arts, via the Israel Academy of Art, by way of the Polish Academy of Art. The story, as told by my mother, went like this:

"New York was in the midst of a full-blown renaissance. Artists, poets, beatniks, musicians, and writers filled the streets. Your father was one of them, always carrying his small easel and art pad under one arm. On the day we met, he was very late to class. He later said he'd had to push through a crowd of students smoking and drinking cof- fee in front of the building to get to the classroom on the top floor.

I was there, standing on a pedestal in all my young, naked, nineteen- year-old glory, making extra money as a nude model. A sheet cov- ered part of my body. I had long, dark, curly hair that fell across my shoulder.

"Your father walked into the loft and found a place at the back of the room. I stood on my pedestal in front of maybe twenty-five artists, some surrounded by swirls of gray cigarette smoke floating in the air, caught by shafts of sunlight. I noticed two pretty painters watching your father as he crossed the floor. One raised her eyebrows at the other, who just smiled and sipped her coffee.

"Richard set up his easel, took out his charcoal, and began to draw. "Meanwhile, Sam, the instructor, did what he always did: he brewed me a cup of tea and looked at his watch. When my time was up, I stepped off the podium, covered myself, and took the tea. Then he asked if I'd like to see the students' work, and together we went from one rendition of myself to another. They were all beautiful.

"But one drawing made me stop. I stared over Richard's shoulder at his work, amazed. But an even more powerful moment occurred when he turned to look at me. I was instantly in love. Why? Because in his eyes I saw my two future children and knew they would be the loves of my life. Beyond anything else, that is why we married.

"I don't know what Richard saw, but in his thick Polish accent he asked, 'Do you like it?'

"'I love it,' I said, unself-consciously wiping away a tear. 'Your line . . . it's sublime.' Richard looked back at his sketch. 'Sublime . . .? This is a good word . . . yes?'

"'Yes, a very good word,' I said."

DEMIAN: My parents moved to Acworth, New Hampshire, and lived on a small horse ranch. Richard bred Appaloosa horses, sculpted, and made linoleum prints. My mother painted. Then one day when I was about two, my mother disappeared for a little while and came back car- rying a crying, snotty little bundle in her arms. She cooed to it and gave it all her attention. When she peeled back the blanket to show me, I met my sister. And to be as Freudian and direct about it as I can, my mother took her breasts out of my mouth and put them into my sister's. In that profoundly and unconsciously disturbing moment I determined that this strange new creature was my enemy, and either she was going to go or I was going to go.

Of course, I had no idea of how to get rid of my sister, so I decided to leave. I just walked out of the house. Remember, I was only two years old. Luckily for me, our German sheepdog, Bosch, went with me down the driveway and followed me onto a dirt road, and then onto a two-lane, paved country highway.

Thus, I was later told, began a frantic search. My parents called the hospitals, the local sheriff, and all their friends. They searched the property, they looked in the wells, they ran all over. And, meanwhile, I was still on my roughly two-and-a-half-mile journey—much of which I actually remember—along the highway until I plopped myself on a neighbor's front lawn.

The neighbors called my parents, and my mother came to get me.

Prior to my sister's arrival, the world was a completely abundant place. It was soft and warm and filled with mother's milk, the nectar of the gods. I was coddled and taken care of, and all my needs and de- sires were met. But then my darling sister arrived, and my special place, my experience of being the most important thing, went away. And then the world became one of lack, scarcity, coldness, and feeling alone. My world was something to be afraid of.

The story is significant because it was the first moment I experienced separateness, a break in my mother and I belonging solely to each other. It became fundamentally clear that the world was no longer just about me. I lost the ability to be the creator of my own existence, though as a two-year-old I certainly didn't think of it in that way. I just felt it. Like people with chronic physical pain, the gnawing emotional pain became the backdrop of my existence.

SHAJEN: If only our parents' marriage had endured. But when I was two and Demian four, they divorced to follow their individual passions. We lived in New Hampshire, but our father went back to New York, and our mother, who had fallen in love with a man who shall remain nameless (who would later become our stepfather), eventually moved us into a house on top of Temple Hill, in the Broad Brook Valley in Vermont. Even so, our parents always told us that whatever had happened, they somehow knew that they had needed

OUR WORLD COMES APART

• • •

SHAJEN: The years passed, and we shuttled between cities and houses and families. We lived with Fonda and our step father during the school year. On vacations we visited our dad in New York City. We were adventurers, enjoying our city status with the local farm kids and our country status with the city kids. Although we were young, we were adept at travel- ing on Amtrak and always loved the epic moment when the conductor yelled, "All aboard!" or "Next stop, New York City!" On the way back we'd hear, "White River Junction, Vermont!" This was our routine.

Yet our lives were about to change again.

Vermont is harsh in winter, and survival on top of a small mountain in the forest requires a very intimate relationship with nature. If you had to keep a fire going in the stove, you were always busy. As children we spent hours chopping, stacking, and hauling wood, as well as becoming experts at fire starting. Sweating and full of splinters, we carried the wood to the house and threw it into a crawl space so small that only children could fit inside. The crawl space was a very dark and scary place, abundant with creatures that scurried or flew in the

9

night, from bats and spiders to squirrels and mice, big black beetles, huge centipedes, and hardwood lice. We didn't look forward to being told, "Get down in the crawl space and throw up some wood."

Still, our home was filled with possibility. We could slide down two flights of stairs on a rope from Demian's bedroom to the kitchen. We had a music room with a piano, drums, guitars, and harmonicas. We also had a two-story greenhouse, a sauna, an eighty-foot deck, and what felt like hundreds of small nooks and crannies waiting for us to explore and play in. We were happy. Our mother loved us. Our home felt like a castle in the sky, in which we imagined we would play forever.

Our mother, Fonda, was vibrant, magnetic, full of zest and enthusiasm. Whenever she walked into a room, everyone would sense the im- mediate surge of energy and turn to look. She was a fearless trailblazer and a woman before her time. She was never afraid of hard work. She raised her children, ran her own business—the Oasis health food store and café, in Woodstock, Vermont—developed real estate, and created statewide arts programs with the Vermont Arts Council. At the same time, she was involved in theater, painting, sculpture, gardening, yoga, and silk screening. She believed in living green and had created a life that followed her values and dreams. In many ways she was living her Gift, yet she lacked one major piece: a partner who could match her energy, compassion, and inspirations.

We were aware of dark undercurrents that lurked in the hearts of our mother and stepfather. Their fights could be explosive. Often we ran into the woods and climbed the ladder to our tree house to escape all the arguing. The inability of these two people—who were both younger than we are now—to see the profound Gift in themselves led to events that would disastrously affect their lives, as well as ours. When adults are not conscious of how unconscious they are, they are unaware of how damaging their actions can be. In many cases the children suffer more than adults realize.

While Demian and I spent winter recess in New York City with our father, Fonda was in emotional turmoil back in Vermont. After many years together, our stepfather, had left her for another woman, an act that left us all disappointed and confused.

Fonda knew it would be tough to make it through the winter with the added burden of keeping up the enormous mountainside house alone. Our family coming apart was like watching a ball of yarn unravel uncontrollably, creating a massive tangled web along the way. The other woman was no surprise for us, as our stepfather had been struggling with monogamy for quite some time. Our lives were changing again and that meant the unknown. Nevertheless, our mom did her best to hold it all together, but on one cold Vermont night in 1981, when I was twelve and Demian was fourteen, our world came undone even more.

Our mother had stepped out of the shower and smelled smoke. Dripping wet, she wrapped a towel quickly around her body and ran into the hallway. She stopped in horror on the walkway suspended over the downstairs kitchen. It wasn't just smoke. It was fire, and it was ev- erywhere. Naked and alone, our mother threw on some clothes and ran downstairs. Smoke stung her eyes and filled her lungs, the flames licked at her hair. Panicked, she began breaking windows and throwing our pos- sessions out of the house into the snow.

We have often imagined what it was like for our mother to stand in the frigid night with the entire mountain lit up by fire and everything she had ever created burning in front of her eyes. And I mean everything we held dear: every family photo, home movie, heirloom. We lost it all. Even the charcoal drawing my father had made on the day he met our mother was gone.

In its place was a blaze that could be seen for twenty miles.

The fire department and paramedics finally arrived and treated Fonda for smoke inhalation and minor burns. It was too late to save the house, so they concentrated on preventing the fire from spreading into the sur- rounding forest.

Back in New York City we were asleep in our beds. We remember our father shaking us to wake up and soon thereafter explaining that our home in Vermont had burned down.

"Is Mom okay?" we asked, almost in the same instant, holding our breaths.

"Yes, she is fine, and she wants to talk to you both." We ran to the phone.

It's a dislocating moment when the world you think most solid and sta- ble is gone, and you realize that all you have left are the few pieces of clothing in your suitcase. It is a strange and hollow feeling as a young mind tries to wrap itself around the impermanence of existence, and the sudden end of life as you knew it. Our home was gone. Vanished. The future was suddenly a big question mark. Demian and I, and our father, talked a lot about what we would do, where we would live, what schools we would attend, what would happen to our friendships. We were anx- ious and didn't know what to expect.

We stayed with our father for a few more days but realized we needed to be at our mother's side. We returned to Vermont. What we found were the charred and still smoking ruins of our previous life, and our mom in a state of traumatic shock and disbelief. Although she'd still been reeling from our step father's leaving, and from raising two kids alone, Fonda now had to focus on the basics of survival. She borrowed clothes and blankets from her friends and tried to figure out her next move.

Fortunately, the townspeople of Sharon stepped up to help in any small way they could. They gave us food and much-needed supplies. Someone even put a glass jar at the local store with our names and pictures, and a note saying we had just lost our house to fire. Fonda's best friends, Jackie and Roger, and their young daughter, Jenny, took us in. They have been like blood family to us ever since. Our plan was to stay with them only until we were able to get a house in Woodstock, where Fonda still had her health food store and café.

DEMIAN: What I remember most about that time was my mother's strength in dealing with bankers, lawyers, insurance companies, her own business, and the sad fact that her lover and partner had recently abandoned her. The weird truth is that Fonda and our stepfather had gone to a marriage counselor . . . and the man we knew as our daily dad, had left my mother for the *marriage counselor.* I remember holding my mother in my fourteen-year-old arms as she sobbed, "My heart is broken . . . my heart is broken . . ."

My mom was an extraordinary and multitalented woman. She was a key member of the Vermont Arts Council; she was an art teacher, a community leader, an activist, a spiritual leader, an herbal shaman. She had a powerful spiritual sense and at the same time was very emotionally driven. And I had to watch the person I loved most in my life go through a devastating heartache.

If she had a fault, I think it was that she obsessed over those whom she loved. Due to the deep wounds of her own childhood she was not ca- pable of letting go, yet letting go was exactly what she needed to do—to surrender to life and have faith that all would be well.

The days swirled together as we attempted to reassemble the pieces of our lives. Everything was up in the air: where we would live, how we would eat, what we would wear, and, most important, how to help Mom. I'll never forget the time the insurance agent came to Jackie and Roger's house to speak with Fonda. During her interview, he asked point-blank if, in fact, she had set the house on fire. They say I leapt from my chair to attack the agent and that he fell backward to get away. I just remember my mom moving fast to knock me down, which she did just in the nick of time.

"You are very lucky that your son did not touch me," the agent said, as Fonda picked me up off the floor.

"No," she said, dusting me off. "You, sir, are the lucky one."

She gave the agent a moment to absorb her admonition, then said, "Now leave and never speak to me again."

The man's insensitivity coupled with our stepfather's betrayal of Fonda were key building blocks in the foundation of what my sister calls my "savior complex." These events were important, but they were not the soon-to-arrive seminal event in which I would realize that I was com- pletely alone in the world.

SHAJEN: Twenty days later, on March 11, 1981, our mother had to work late at the Oasis. After closing up, she stopped by a favorite res- taurant, Bentley's, just down the street from her café. She hung out with some friends, then started the long drive home.

Because Jackie, Roger, and Jenny were on vacation, Demian and I were spending the night with friends. I was at my friend Chrissie's house. At one-thirty in the morning, her father woke me and asked me to come downstairs to talk with him. In the middle of the night? I was terri- fied. Suddenly I had a flashback of an ugly experience with a different friend's father who had sexually abused me. But that was another night, in another strange home, six years earlier—and I'd told no one about it. Chrissie's father was a kind and gentle man, but still I refused to move. Finally, he sent his wife upstairs to get me. I remember her footsteps in the hallway. She came in and asked me to come downstairs. I still refused, so she sat on the bed, hugged me, and said, "Your mom just died. The rescue squad picked her up, but they couldn't save her. I am so sorry. Please come downstairs with me now."

Chrissie's mother was the head of the local rescue squad, and she'd gotten the call and sent her team out on a bitter winter night when the black ice of a frozen road and the strength of a single small ash tree would end our mother's life.

They found my mother's car smashed against that tree on Lower Broad Brook Road, only two miles from Jackie and Roger's house, just a few minutes from her bed and the rest she desperately needed. They told me she'd died instantly . . . but I know that's also what they say when the truth is too much to bear.

While the rescue squad took care of Fonda, Chrissie's mom stayed home to watch over me and gather my brother.

I remember throwing up after I heard the news. Then I called Demian, who was at his friend's house, and told him, "Mommy is dead." I will never forget his words that night. "I know," he said. "I heard the town sirens earlier, and I knew it was Mom."

DEMIAN: I was at my friend Michael's house. I remember it was late that night and I was drawing a picture of a pterodactyl attacking another dinosaur that was eating another pterodactyl. I remember sketching the thigh muscle on the dinosaur when suddenly I felt a ping, like a pull, like a pop in my heart. I looked out the windows and saw the cold moon reflecting off the mountainside covered in snow. But instead of feeling its beauty, I felt a sudden and profound sense of loss, of separation. A few minutes later the town siren went off, and then a few minutes later the phone rang. It was Chrissie's mom.

Michael picked up the phone, said nothing, and hung up. He walked over to me and said, "You have to get ready. Somebody is coming to get you." I said, "It's about my mom, isn't it?"

"I'm not supposed to say anything."

"You're my best friend. You can tell me. It's about my mom, isn't it?" His body and eyes answered my question.

"She's dead, isn't she?" He said yes.

My mother was thirty-eight years old.

Then the phone rang again. It was my sister. I then remember bend- ing down to tie my shoelaces, but I couldn't. I'd forgotten how. Michael bent down and tied them for me. I didn't cry then. All I could think about was getting to Shajen. Soon thereafter the police picked me up and brought me to her.

SHAJEN: It sounds strange, but I'd also had that empty, separated feel- ing. Earlier that evening I'd been scared and called my mother and told her I had "a bad feeling in my tummy." For some reason I told her to stay at the Oasis that night, where we had a small apartment above the café.

"It's okay, sweetheart," she'd said. "Dream of roses and I will see you in the morning."

Someone had to tell our father. I called and he promised to be on the next plane out of the city. Then I kept busy by calling Mom's friends whose phone numbers I remembered. Eight hours later I found myself in my father's arms, devastated, confused, and in shock.

DEMIAN: We all have those moments that change our lives. That one changed mine forever. I knew everything would be different now. I had to take care of my sister. I had to man up really fast and handle a lot of stuff. At fourteen years old I suddenly found myself the proverbial man of the family. My sister was absolutely devastated. Everything that seemed real to me was gone. And when I say "everything," I mean every photograph, every movie, every picture, every drawing, every painting, every memory, all of it burnt to the ground . . . and now, my mother dead. I had to identify the car, and I had to see what had happened to her in that car. That was the toughest thing I ever had to do.

My mother taught me many, many great lessons, and eventually, as I got older, I was able to take the power of those lessons and move forward in my life. But as a teenager, I didn't really understand how to manage my anger. Instead, I was big, strong, young, and filled with rage.

Thank God for my father. He loved us profoundly and deeply, and if not for him we might not have been able to navigate what lay ahead. We couldn't have known it at the time, but we were about to receive an enormous Gift: our father's unwavering support and uncon- ditional love.

We would need it.

I don't know how many people came to the funeral, but there seemed to be so many that it was unbelievable. We lowered my mother's casket into the ground in Broad Brook Cemetery, which also happened to be the name of the road she died on. The rabbi spoke, and then it was time to shovel the dirt in. They gave me the shovel first. I started shovel- ing . . . and I didn't stop. I shoveled until my hands bled and finally some- one put his hands on my shoulders and said it was time to stop. I think I did that because I wanted to bury the pain as fast as I could. So, hands bloody, I looked at the sea of people, made eye contact with as many of them as I could, only to see them drop their heads and turn away. I said, "Where were all of you?"

At that moment Jackie embraced me and said, "From now on I'm your mother." And she did a great job.

SHAJEN: The whole experience was strange and disorienting. I felt like I was watching myself in a movie. At her grave, I looked up to see my brother unable to stop shoveling the dirt.

Every Mother's Day we plant flowers around her little red granite gravestone, the one with the single red rose, in honor of her. Often we have thought of getting her a much grander and bigger stone to mark her place, but that little red stone has so much meaning, and that is still yet another story.

DEMIAN: I felt lost and spent a lot of time away from Shajen. I re- member, shortly after my mother died, I walked up Temple Hill. I lay down at the top and looked up at the sky, and I allowed myself to liter- ally leave my body. I soared into space, into the cosmos. I experienced infinity. I understood it, I grasped it—the infinity feedback loop of cre- ation, though I wouldn't have used those words at the time. I became frightened. Suddenly I felt my spirit racing back through the cosmos, hurtling into the Milky Way, sailing past planets, past the moon, break- ing through the cloud layer, slamming through the atmosphere, and *bam!* right back into my body.

Safe to say, I knew my life would never be the same. I had to find my way in the world. I had a job to do. I didn't know what it was then, but soon it became clear: to be an expert filmmaker. It was spring. I left town, immediately moved in with my father in the SoHo section of New York, and went to the High School of Art and Design to study motion pictures, television, and photography. Shajen stayed in Vermont for the remainder of the school year and joined us later that summer in the city.

SHAJEN: After Fonda's death and then moving to New York, life only got more difficult for me. Where once Demian and I had stood together, we now had opposite reactions to all that had happened. The farther apart we grew, the more difficult it was for me to grasp why Demian seemed to love his friends, but not me.

The only time I really got his attention was when he was angry with me. He clearly disapproved of me. I was too fat. Everything I said an- noyed him. According to Demian, all my friends were hippies and he didn't like that. I wanted a loving relationship like we'd once had, but he wasn't interested. Instead he fired arrows into my heart.

Too often his anger would turn to rage, which while not good in any situation, was particularly tough for a young girl who had been brought up to speak her mind, and to believe that what she had to say was important.

As our relationship continued to deteriorate because of Demian's anger toward me, I began to withdraw from the family. I quit high school when I turned fifteen. I couldn't see any point in that type of education, as it held no meaning for my fractured spirit. Not one teacher reached out to me. Instead I got my GED and began working full-time as a wait- ress at an artists' café in SoHo.

This job would be my salvation for the next two years. Because I wasn't in school any longer, my friends and I drifted apart, and I began to connect with the café's transient waitstaff, folks from all over the world. My closest friend at the time was a wonderful young man from Tuni- sia named Amor. He would listen to my stories of confusion and pain regarding my relationship with Demian. He couldn't understand why I put up with it. But I felt paralyzed and unable to shift my reality. Since I had moved to New York with Demian and my father, my life seemed to decline rapidly.

By the time I was seventeen, Demian's rage at me was so violent that I feared for myself physically. My boyfriend at the time, Jerry, and Demian's friend Charles stood by as Demian's face grew red, his voice shrill, his posture poised to attack and about to lose control. I was so shocked I just stood there like a movie character paralyzed at the sight of a train bearing down. Suddenly my father stood between us. Even though I'd complained about it often, he had never actually witnessed Demian lose his temper at me before. Perhaps he was in denial.

At that moment I knew I was through. This would be the last time I let this happen. I'd never again allow Demian's anger to touch my soul. I realized that the only place I'd feel safe was back home in the mountains of Vermont. I left our home in SoHo that day and moved north to heal my wounds.

I was seventeen. Jackie and Roger welcomed me with open arms. Their love and consistency gave me a foundation and a home. I felt safe. I could even share my pain, anger, and confusion about the events of my life.

I had always been interested in personal development, yoga, and al- ternative ways of living that were just a little different than the main- stream. Jackie took me to an alternative college in the hills of Vermont, called Goddard College. There I found my true nature and the beginning of life as I know it today. Thanks to taking that one small instinctive step—returning to Vermont—part of my life was reborn. As hard as it was to leave my father, removing the immediate obstacles to my growth gave me personal power and the energy to continue. I wouldn't have called it this then, but I became the creator of my world.

The 1980s were full of powerful lessons for me. My life had been tumultuous, and I was an emotional basket case who repressed my feelings of imperfection and attachment to everything that was wrong with me. Trying to stumble my way through adolescence without my mother was hard enough. But having to endure the anger of my older brother was the final straw. What I didn't know then was that this was a life lesson that would later feed my passions and ultimately be a major factor in creating one of my most valuable Gifts: a deep connection with children and family.

As I have come to learn, Gifts are found in all circumstances.

DEMIAN: I want to rewind a bit and tell you a little about my early years before tragedy struck, because as it turns out, I had a very early re- lationship with the frame. What do I mean by "the frame"? Well, let me tell you.

When I was really young, my mother found me sitting on a canvas, freshly painted white. I had stuck a brush in some ink and painted a frame around myself. My mom later showed me a photo of that moment. When I was about seven, she started teaching me photography. She took me to the top of Temple Hill and set up the Canon camera on a tri- pod. Then she told me to pick my first lens. I chose a 135-mm portrait lens, snapped it into the camera, and put my eye to the viewfinder to find a frame. I looked at the mountain and the trees, at a moss-covered rock wall, at the deer eating in the apple orchard about a hundred yards away.

I looked at a farm on the opposite side of the valley. Then I turned away from the lens.

"What's wrong?" she asked.

"Nothing is wrong. It's just all so beautiful, I don't know what pho- tograph to take first. What if I take the wrong one?"

"Oh, I see," she said. "Okay. I'm going to tell you something, and I want you to remember it for the rest of your life because it doesn't only relate to photography, okay?"

"Okay."

She leaned in close. "What you leave outside of the frame is just as important as what you put in the frame."

Suddenly the wind kicked up and the sun shone through the clouds. I pointed the camera at my mother. She smiled and I took my first photograph.

From there I ended up becoming a punk, precocious off-Broadway child actor. I did a play called *The Informer*. It was set in Nazi Germany and was about German parents who were anti-Hitler, even though they weren't Jewish, and who believe their son might be part of the Hitler Youth because the boy across the street was, and the boy next door was—and those sons had turned in their parents for being against Hitler. And even though the child doesn't know what's happening, he starts to understand that he has all the power.

It was very interesting for me as a Jewish kid to play the Gentile son of anti-Nazi parents, when quite a few of my own family did not survive the Holocaust.

Of course, I instantly disagreed with the director. Poor guy. After I voiced my opinion, he pulled me aside and said, "Listen, kid, when you're the director, you can do it any way you want. Until then, get on stage and do it the way I told you."

I went home that night and announced to my family that I was now a director. Everyone just looked at me.

Back in the country, I was a bit of a wild child, running around Temple Hill with the crazy farm kids in the neighborhood. But I also liked to build models of planes and tanks and then create dioramas. Sometimes I'd spend months setting up these static scenes—only to empty the gunpow- der from some shotgun shells, make a little bomb, and watch it all blow up. Around the third or fourth time, as my mom picked plastic splinters out of my face with her tweezers, she came up with a plan to save me from hurting myself. She bought me a Bell & Howell Super 8 camera. "Look, I know you're building another model, and I know you are going to blow it up," she said. "No, I'm not."

She gave me a "you can't fool me" smile and said, "I know you. You are. It's all right. But here's an idea. Take this camera and mount it on the tripod. Stand far away and use the zoom, and shoot what happens. You'll be protected because one eye will be looking through the lens and the other eye will be closed while you're focusing."

My mother's plan to save my eyes started me off as a filmmaker.

When I finally moved back to New York, I made it into the very presti- gious High School of Art and Design. I graduated a top film and tele- vision student in New York City in 1984. I was blessed to receive the Helena Rubinstein scholarship to New York University, where I went to study film and business because, even then, I always understood it was the film *business*. I did an accelerated program and won awards for videos on MTV and for best action director at NYU.

All this was wonderful, but in the midst of success, another major event forced me to construct more walls to guard my heart.

Right before going to NYU's film school, my first serious girlfriend, Heather, committed suicide. She was sixteen, from Modesto, California, and attended private school on the East Coast. She went home for a visit, and her mother found her in her room overdosed. This happened just a couple of years after my mother had died in the car wreck. Heather was the first girl—woman—to whom I had given my heart since that tragedy.

I didn't intellectualize it at the time, but somehow deep down I got the idea that the women I loved would die—*because I loved them*. What I did, but couldn't see then, was to distance myself from my sister, because if I could act like I didn't love her, she would live.

SHAJEN: In some ways, like Demian, I believe that losing my mother was also the beginning of my professional journey. What began as leaving high school at fifteen turned into a passion for creating safe environments for "at risk" youth (the so-called freaks, loners, and outsiders), students seeking to understand themselves and the worlds they lived in, and families who've undergone traumas and are struggling emotionally.

Today, as an educator, school counselor, and school administrator, I have worked with thousands of students and their families. I believe that when a student is in trouble, it usually leads to a parent or family system in need of support and repair. The Gift I bring to others came to me out of adversity. I endured and blossomed because—although I didn't use this terminology—I instinctively looked for the Gift in any situation. When I was younger, I called those Gifts "blessings in disguise."

This ability was natural, and I believe it came from knowing deep inside of me what I needed to do to heal. My mother had always told me how important it is to listen to myself, to cry when I need to cry, and to laugh when I need to laugh. Her wisdom was so profound and so penetrating that I never forgot any of her important life lessons, and they have always served me well.

A DEFINING MOMENT

• • •

DEMIAN: If you took a snapshot of my life in New York City in the late 1980s and early 1990s, to many people it would look perfect. I lived in a beautiful SoHo loft. I drove a white Jaguar. I had beautiful girl- friends. I ran my own business. In my little world I was, if not famous, at least notorious.

But as I made professional progress, I began to hide behind layers and layers of emotional baggage. I didn't want to chance feeling any pain, like I had when I was younger. My ego and arrogance grew. So did my anger. I didn't do this intentionally, but I let it happen so I wouldn't be vulnerable.

But no matter how often I'd look into the mirror and see a success- ful guy, I knew something was missing. And it was missing to such a degree that I was scared. And it didn't matter what I did to fill in the empty space. I tried it all: drugs, alcohol, women, parties, rock 'n' roll. I did whatever I could to distract myself from the pain I couldn't name. Even if I thought, okay, it's because of my mom dying, or the house burning, or the girlfriend committing suicide, or whatever—that solved nothing.

If anything, I was conscious enough to know that I was deeply unconscious.

So in October of 1994 I picked up the phone, dialed my friend Eric, who lived in Los Angeles, and made what we have termed "that call."

When Eric answered the phone, I said, "This is 'that call.'" "That call?"

"Yeah, that call."

Eric said, "Okay. Where are you?" "In my loft in New York City."

"Okay," he said. "Well, get on the next plane to L.A."

It was three in the morning, a moment of pure desperation, so I did what he suggested. I drove my car to JFK and parked at the sidewalk in front of the terminal—I'm sure you can't do that anymore, but back then you could. I left the keys in the car, and a note that I would pick it up from the impound when I got back. Then I flew to L.A.

When Eric met me, I asked, "Now what do I do?" He said, "It's time for you to wake up."

"How do I do that?"

Eric explained that he wanted me to take a self-improvement seminar. I agreed, and two weeks later I was sitting in an auditorium arguing— as was my habit—with one of the instructors about how I was right about something and she was wrong and didn't know what she was talk- ing about.

When I finally shut up, she said, "Can I ask you a question?"

I said, "Sure."

"Do you have a sister? Let's talk about your sister."

Sister? Where did that question come from? But I didn't want to go there. "I didn't come here to talk about her," I snapped. "I came here to talk about me."

The whole room got quiet.

The leader said, "Well, I think maybe your sister is exactly who you should talk about."

I said, "I told you already, I didn't come here to talk about her. I came here to talk about me."

"Well," she said, as if there were no alternative, "we're going to talk about you and your sister."

"But I'm not interested," I said. "We'll talk about what I want to talk about."

"You know, Demian," she continued, "you're here for many reasons, one of which is that your life isn't working the way you've been running it." She paused to let that sink in. "But I have something that I think you might want, and I would like to share that with you."

"Really, Beth? What is that?"

She said, "The reason you are so profoundly unhappy, even with all of your success, even with your understanding of the death of your mother—and, yes, your first girlfriend committed suicide, and, yes, this happened, and, yes, that happened—the reason you're so profoundly un- happy is because you have no relationship with one of your two closest living blood relatives. Your sister."

All right, she had a point, but I wasn't about to give in that easily. I said, "You know, Beth, that is about the biggest load of horsesh—" and she cut me off.

"Demian, I think you should sit down and be quiet and just listen for a little while. I'm going to throw it out there, and, like a hat, if it fits, wear it. If not, then take it off."

"Okay," I said. "Do it."

She said, "The hat is that your entire life will transform when you understand that the relationship you *do not* have is going to change your entire existence when you actually engage in transforming your relation- ship with your sister."

I still didn't believe a word she said, but I stayed seated, shut my mouth, and, since I'd paid my money, kept that hat on.

Three days later, in the middle of an exercise, in a blinding flash of insight, I stood up during the seminar and walked out.

My life had looked perfect. But I wasn't satisfied.

As I said, I was missing something, the presence of which I abso- lutely believed would make a profound difference in my life.

If only I could find it.

This much I knew: I had not suspected until that moment that hav- ing no relationship with my sister could be affecting me so profoundly. And why was that? Because of me. I realized that I was the source of the fighting in my family.

I had to find a pay phone. (In 1994 we didn't all carry cell phones.) When I found one, I called Shajen, expecting to leave a message on her answering machine. But her best friend, Jenna, picked up, gave her the phone, and the moment I heard her voice, I started to sob.

After that moment of reconnecting with Shajen, the vibrational shift in energy between my sister and me was so profound that it permeated our entire family. We all stopped fighting! This taste of peace and freedom and love created a desire in me to continue this journey of personal and spiritual awakening.

I plunged into years of deep transformational study and work. I be- came hungry for this new knowledge, hungry to learn about myself in ways I had never known existed. I went to seminar after seminar after seminar. I did men's work. I did group therapy. I did American Indian sweat lodges. I did sacred movement and dance. I studied healing meta- physics. I studied the body, the mind, the soul, the spirit.

I've never believed in God as an all-encompassing being, an old white man with a flowing beard sitting on a cloud passing judgment on hu- manity. However, I did believe, and believe now even more, in a universal spirit that permeates all existence. Now aware of that spirit, I continued to work in the arena of my Gift as a storyteller and filmmaker—but with a different purpose and point of view. Instead of thinking I knew it all, I sought out those who had a much broader understanding of life than I did. I learned a lot and slowly began my personal transformation from what I was to what I am today.

Conventional wisdom holds that if you want to become successful at something, don't reinvent the wheel. Instead, seek out a mentor with whom you resonate, and make yourself available to them, as a student to a teacher. As a filmmaker, I sought out someone for whom I had the greatest respect: James Cameron.

James Cameron directed *Avatar, Titanic, Terminator,* and many more movies. To me he is one of the greatest filmmakers alive today. I had the profound privilege of being able to work and train with him for a very short, yet eye-opening time, when he was making *Avatar.* That in- tense experience helped shift me into who I am today. What I also dis- covered is that people like James Cameron, who have mastered their own Gift, *want to share it*—not hoard it. They want to give it away; they want other people to understand what it is that they have learned.

It is as simple as this: Imagine wanting to hike up a mountain. You meet an ancient mountain man at the bottom, fishing in the lake. You wave and take the path around the left side of the lake. The old man asks, "Where are you going?"

"To climb the mountain."

He says, "Take the right path instead of the left path." "Why?"

And he says, "Because the right path will lead you there and the left path won't."

Ten years ago, in 2001, I found myself at a place actually called the "Mountain of Attention," a sanctuary and hermitage in Northern Cali-fornia. I was sitting in front of one of the most extraordinary spiritual teachers I had ever encountered. His name was Adi Da. What he ex- plained to me was that I had a purpose on this planet, which was to use the extraordinary Gifts I had as a storyteller to help spread light to the world. He said that in the not-too-distant future the combination of technology and my Gifts would make that possible. I was convinced he was talking to the wrong guy. Truth be told, who I was at that time was not yet capable of doing any of that. But now it is clear that he was right about me. What had happened is I had met the proverbial man at the mountain, and he told me which path to take.

It took some time, but *Discover the Gift* is that right path, and in shar- ing that path, I am 100 percent going for my dream. My dream is not only to be the best filmmaker I can be, but the best at sharing the dis- coveries I've made in my life. I want to live my Gift and be of service to my family, my friends, my teachers, and most of all this precious world of ours.

So far, so good. I'm learning every day. I am transforming in ways I never even thought possible. But I realized that if I wanted to tell a story of transformation, I had to look at everything standing between me and my own continuing transformation. All of it.

I came to realize I had to discard some personal habits and ways of being. I've become very conscious of the power and ways in which I af- fect others, and I never want to abuse that. And so I'm constantly work- ing on being present to my presence—meaning being aware of who and how I am being at any given moment. If I want deep connections and relationships with those I love, then being able to be conscious and aware of which patterns, beliefs, and habits are serving that purpose is crucial in my own development. Don't we want the deepest and most profound relationship that we can have with the people in our lives who mean the most to us?

That's what I want. When we come into the world, it seems that we are all promised a share of joy, of pain, of transformative experiences—and it all ends with the guarantee of death. And very few people on their deathbed have said, "God, I just wish I had bought one more toy, or taken one more trip."

As life comes to an end, we assess instead our relationships and our capacity to love. And we ask ourselves: "Did we do those things as well as possible?"

Discovering the Gift, discovering *your* Gift, and sharing it with your- self and the world will, I promise you, make the answer to that ultimate question a brilliant YES.

SHAJEN AND DEMIAN: We trust that reading this story has given you insight into some of what we have encountered in our lives, and what we needed to move through in order to discover the Gift for ourselves. We know that we left a great deal of our history out, and that we are not alone in having experienced emotional pain and hardship. But like all those people who went before us and inspire us now, we continue to find value in our journey. This book is not meant to aggrandize or dramatize our lives or in any way make our story more significant than anyone else's. It is presented to reveal background on and context to the personal journeys that resulted in *Discover the Gift*.

We're happy to say that despite life's wounds, we've rediscovered each other's hearts and re-created our family. Everyone has a story, and ours led us to experience the extraordinary, powerful transformation we will now share with you.

PART TWO

Eight Steps to

Discovering and

Unfolding Your

Gift

A REVELATION

. . .

DEMIAN: A few years ago I had a flash of transformation and a big breakthrough moment with my sister. Suddenly I popped into a new world. I felt alive. I felt connected to everything. I could see, touch, smell, and hear things in a way I hadn't before. I marveled at the wonders of life and suddenly thought that I knew something about nature and God and the divine spirit.

And then I experienced another flash: the revelation of a system of harmonious principles—eight distinct universal spiritual steps all working together in a unified field of consciousness. They came in fast: receptivity, intention, activation, feedback, vibration, adversity and transformation, compassion, and love. I was in a state of bliss, I had experienced something that was important for my evolution. It became clear that I needed to change on levels that were deeper than I had ever imagined.

And then suddenly, in this open space, every bad habit and overblown piece of my ego came rushing back in to fill this new space I'd just cre- ated. I felt like I was back to square one—or worse—because now I knew that the unified field existed.

If I wanted my understanding of these principles to evolve, I real- ized I would have to work hard for it, earn it. I would have to pursue it like my life depended on it—and to me, it did. My friend Chet Holmes introduced me to Michael and Sydney Cresci, who were hosting a sym- posium on consciousness attended by authors, motivational speakers, and transformational leaders from around the world. They had come together to embark on an epic journey to the frontier of what is possible in personal growth. The subject was how each of us can make a differ- ence in our own lives and on the planet. They shared lifetimes' worth of knowledge from their hearts.

I knew I was ready for something, but I was totally unprepared for the adventure that was about to begin. Little by little, through study and observation, my life began to change and I was never the same again.

Everyone has a Gift to give. We believe we are on this life journey to acquire new knowledge and new ways of being that will support us along the next phase of our existence. Barbara De Angelis states, "We're here to learn. There's a curriculum. We each have certain courses. You can actually figure out your courses if you look at the experiences in your life."

DEMIAN'S PERSPECTIVE

The human mind is very complex. We are pattern recognition machines, constantly predicting the next event that might possibly happen to us based on what has happened to us before. Our evolutionary patterns create this automatic response and this response comes from millennia of conditioning from the perspective that survival was at stake and was all that mattered. You walked out of the cave and you needed to know if that shadow in the distance was a saber-tooth tiger ready to leap out and drag you off and eat you. Or was it just a tree?

Although thousands of years have passed and we no longer live in caves or fear being eaten by wild animals (at least here in most of the United States), similar kinds of conditioned response patterns still exist on our deepest levels. Only now the patterns reflect our modern cir- cumstances. For example, when you cross the street, your brain subcon- sciously scans the area for warning signs that a car might be bearing down on you.

In fact, the way we respond to everything that happens to us is actu- ally based on previous patterns already in our mind. Said simply, if you were trapped inside a room and didn't know the pattern for a door, you wouldn't recognize a way to get out.

We are also constantly conditioned by our emotions, which are very powerful tools that can guide us toward the fulfillment we can find in discovering our Gift.

Think about an emotion, such as joy or happiness, and ask yourself, "When do I most feel joy and happiness, a sense of profound fulfill- ment?" Pinpoint when it happens for you. For me, it mostly occurs when I'm directing a movie or when I'm spending time with my family or my best friends. It also happens when I'm learning something new or trans- forming myself to a new level.

I follow my emotions because they are messages or signposts that guide me toward what I really want in my life.

We are conditioned by culture, by the media, by our family histories. I recently met a man who had been of service to people his entire life. He literally risked his life every day to save other people's lives. Yet he was a very angry man. He had four sons. His new wife told me that he treated his sons very harshly, in the same way that his own father had treated him.

Why? Simple. The man was conditioned. This was his way. It felt natural and necessary. It made emotional sense. He never questioned his actions. They seemed right. After all, his father had done the same, and even though the man didn't like how his father had treated him, in the end he'd turned out okay. So it couldn't hurt to be tough with his own kids. Right?

Maybe. But he was also passing on behavior he hadn't liked and was making it possible for his sons to treat their own families that way.

If we want to transform our lives, we have to break the cycle of limit- ing ideas and actions we have been conditioned to believe.

Conditioned ideas can be seen in religions. Dogmatic religious views are dogmatic because some authority has said, "This is just the way it is. This is the only way for you to speak to God, the only way you can experience the divine, the only pathway to heaven."

But consider this. Just because a belief is conditioned into us—or some authority figure says, "This is the only way"—doesn't mean it's the truth. It's not necessarily supported by the facts. It's not reality; it's just a belief. I'm not saying beliefs are wrong in and of themselves, but I am saying that they are just *beliefs* and that if we understand them as such, our minds will be more receptive to new ideas.

Here's something I believe in: unity consciousness. What's that?, you might be asking. It's a quantum physics concept reflecting the idea that we are all just part of a unified field of energy. Put more spiritually, we are all part of a divine essence, and once we realize this we are one step closer to discovering our Gift and sharing it with the world.

Earlier on, I mentioned something I like to call the infinity feedback loop of creation. Let me explain this concept a little more. Our relation- ship to the Infinite, to that divine essence, is constant. We are all part of it. It's like each part of us is a musician in a symphony. We can, on our own, make beautiful music. But working together, we can make that beautiful music so powerful it can blow the roofs off buildings. Now just as a musical note vibrates and has pitch, each of our actions carries with it a particular energy vibration. Some of our actions harmonize with other actions, and some don't. Now what's really interesting is that when we begin following the path to our Gift, we can focus on the vibra- tions that harmonize most completely with the universe, and that music ends up changing our lives. Not to mention it changes the lives of others who send out their Gift vibrations, which harmonize with ours and so on and so on. We get back what we share. Perpetually. In fact, we can't do anything else.

As with everything, there is equilibrium. When you start on your path to discover the Gift within yourself, one of the first things you no- tice is that the biggest obstacle on this journey is *you*.

How is that possible?

Your belief systems, your mind, your emotions, your established pat- terns can get in the way. Often those patterns would just like to stay as they are, vibrating as always. They don't want to change, because then they would cease to exist. They wouldn't be patterns anymore. They'd just be dispersed energy.

But if your emotions are telling you that you are not who you want to be, you have to break your patterns and develop new thought processes. How do you do this? First, you have to open yourself to the possibil-ity that there might be something extraordinary for you to learn. There might be a *new* possibility that you never thought of before. And even better: it's there for you to discover so that you can move powerfully into the life you are here to have. We promise you there is a reason. We prom- ise you that you have something extraordinary to share with the world that is as unique as your fingerprint, as unique as every snowflake.

You are a divine emanation of the universal energy, and you are here to express who you are. It is in that self-expression, in actively leading yourself down new pathways, that you will find your true power.

And when that happens, you will be transformed.

SHAJEN'S PERSPECTIVE

Our mind, our emotions, and our conditioning are the core of how we behave, what we believe, and thus the source of our viewpoint on life. What I have learned since studying human development, psychology, and spirituality is we *do* have choices in the direction of our life's out- come if we choose to believe that choice is possible.

The first step is to get to know ourselves, and to be open to personal evolution and trans- formation. You are only stuck when you choose to be stuck. I know it doesn't appear that way, that some outside force seems to hold you in a place you don't want to be, but that's not true. When we transform our- selves, we transform the world.

Each step outlined here in *Discover the Gift* has a distinct impact upon our everyday life. The more you understand the dynamics of each step, the better chance you have at arriving at your destination. So let's look at the eight steps again:

1. Receptivity
2. Intention
3. Activation
4. Infinite Feedback
5. Vibration
6. Adversity and Transformation
7. Creating a Conscious and Compassionate World
8. Love—The Ultimate Gift

The eight steps I glimpsed some years back encompass the emotional and spiritual spectrum of our lives. When we discover our Gifts, we are inevitably inspired to express them, to share them and to become them. This process can be brief, fully activating within days or weeks, or it can take years for your beautiful Gifts to truly shine through. But either way, this process unfolds along similar lines. We present the steps here in a lin- ear fashion, but it is important to know that we all grow in unique kinds of directions. We could look at the steps in the reverse order to get an- other picture of how they work together. For instance, Step 8 is love, and coming from that place, we can see adversity not as a bad thing, but as a Gift for growth. Just because someone objects to something we do and we don't get what we want, it doesn't have to be a negative experience—if that objection comes from a place of compassion and love.

So remember that the eight steps are always working in conjunction with one another. We break them apart to carefully examine each one here, but as you get used to the rhythms of consciously participating in your own journey, they will appear as one again. Think about how light works. We know that when we shine white light through a prism we see a rainbow. The prism refracts the light into a spectrum, separating each individual color and reflecting a distinct rainbow pattern. The colors ap- pear in a very specific order every time. The pattern of the rainbow is always the same. They always go from red to purple. Yet blended together these same colors make white light again.

The eight steps are like those very distinct layers and when you incor- porate all the steps together in your daily life, you reach a state of unity, of equilibrium, of love. You become the light. You become a Gift to the world. When this consciously directed blending takes place, your bur- dens become lighter and your energy increases dramatically, because you no longer carry around the weight of your old patterns and the history they wrought. You reach a state of personal balance we call "being pres- ent to your own presence." You feel more in tune with yourself—more aerodynamic and agile, capable of making decisions and choices that bring happiness to your life. Your life becomes a sleek surfboard that lets you move effortlessly through the oceans of life, making course correc- tions and adjustments as needed without blame, shame, or upset.

As we approach the first of the eight steps, we have asked our guides and teachers to provide insight for each step along the way. They are a wise, re- nowned, and accomplished group—so accomplished, in fact, that to give their complete résumés would take much space. For now, we have used only their names—many of which you may immediately recognize—and we humbly ask you to turn to "Contributor Biographies" at the end of the book for more information on their backgrounds.

Each step also has an accompanying mandala, a reproduction of which is contained in the insert of this book. These mandalas are offered here as a source of inspiration and meditation. As His Holiness the Dalai Lama explains, "I think a channel to reach the mind is the drawing of the man- dalas, because the visual impression is a very, very influential way to express deep feelings and deep awareness, and to develop the values of compassion and forgiveness." Moreover, the mandalas represent for us the chakras, or energy centers, that exist in certain parts of our bodies. When these cen- ters are open and moving freely, we experience great amounts of energy and well-being. When they are moving slowly, or if they are closed, they make us feel drained. Here is a brief overview of the basic chakra system and their corresponding mandalas, as shown in the book's color insert:

Red Mandala, Root Chakra

Located at the base of the spine, the root chakra represents earth, sur- vival, security, fluidity, patience, grounding, and stillness.

Orange Mandala, Second Chakra

The sacral chakra is located just beneath the navel and is related to our sexuality and reproductive systems. This chakra is responsible for our relationships, fantasies, and sensuality.

Yellow Mandala, Third Chakra

Located at the area of the solar plexus, this chakra controls our personal power.

Green Mandala, Fourth Chakra

The heart chakra is the center of all chakras and the place that connects the lower and higher energies of the body. This chakra is responsible for unconditional love, affinity, compassion, healing presence, harmony, and air.

Blue Mandala, Fifth Chakra

Located at the throat, this chakra is responsible for communication and the expression of our knowledge and imagination.

Indigo Mandala, Sixth Chakra

The third-eye chakra channels our true vision and allows us to gaze up- ward toward the divine, as well as looking inward into the inner world of our self.

Violet Mandala, Seventh Chakra

The crown chakra connects us to divine truth and higher consciousness and when it is open can bring us closer to our spiritual self, provide guid- ance, wisdom, and inner strength.

The Unified Field of Love

If you turn to the last page of the color insert, you will find a beautiful painting unifing all the chakras and mandalas in the realm of our hu- manity. When all the chakras are open and working correctly, we experi- ence harmony. We experience love. It's why we're here.

As we unlock the eight steps in *Discover the Gift,* your awareness and observations will do wonders for cleansing and opening these centers. You can find an example of how these mandalas and centers align in the Step 8 illustration in the color insert, as well as in the last exercise in this book.

Before you continue reading, we encourage you to pause and become present to your presence. Take a deep breath, breathe in gratitude, and allow it to permeate every cell of your being. As you release your breath, breathe out any negative emotions or thoughts you have been holding on to. With your next breath, breathe in light and love; as you exhale, breathe out anger, confusion, and darkness. As you're doing this, become aware of your body, your mind, and emotions. How does your back feel? Are your shoulders tense or loose? What are you thinking about? What mental movies are playing in your mind? What are you feeling in your heart? Happiness? Contentment? Anxiety? Fear? Become conscious of all these things and continue to breathe in goodness and gratitude while breathing out negativity and confusion. You may find your mind racing around from one idea or feeling or experience to another.

This is okay. Just observe what's going on inside you. Try not to judge yourself (though we know from experience that's a lot easier said than done). Do this for a few minutes or as long as you feel comfortable and come back to this simple technique throughout your day. Daily practice will help clear a path for your inner Gift to manifest itself.

Know that you are on the right path because this is where you are now, and you can accomplish anything you desire through this kind of personal awareness and discovery: how you are feeling, what you are thinking, and how you are reflecting on your own thinking and being. Your *source,* your inner wisdom, is constantly speaking to you. The more you are able to be present and tune in to your source— your inner wisdom, your soul—and the more you are able to act on this *inner knowl- edge,* the more joyful your life will be.

What we have learned over the years of intensive study and experi- mentation, is that our journey in this life is about self-understanding, self-appreciation, and acceptance. The more we are able to love and ac- cept ourselves, the more we are able to love and accept others. Love is the ultimate essence for which we all strive, whether we are aware of it or not. Our lives are made up of many peaks and valleys, and it is at the heart of these peaks and valleys that our true and unique nature resides.

So, without further ado, let's begin.

STEP 1: RECEPTIVITY

Red Mandala
Receptivity and Flexibility = Red Lotus Sparkles

•   •   •

You know life itself is a Gift and it comes with a beautiful wrapping paper. But sometimes we are so caught up in the glittery wrapping paper that we stay at the surface. We never unwrap. We never explore the depths of what life is. We need to unwrap the Gifts that life offers and discover really what is inside of us.

One obstacle to unwrapping the Gift is self-blame. It's as if the wrapping paper is dirty and so we discard the Gift inside, assuming it's no good. And yet if we unwrapped the Gift we might find something very precious indeed. When you want to discover the Gift that nature has given to you, you must first stop blaming yourself for being who you are.

— HIS HOLINESS
SRI SRIR AVI SHANKAR

Each person comes into this world with a specific destiny— he has something to fulfill, some message has to be delivered, some work has to be completed. You are not here accidentally—you are here meaningfully. There is a purpose behind you. The whole intends to do something through you.

— OSHO

The first step we'd like to talk about is receptivity. It is about being open to all possibilities and allowing yourself to grow in the direction of those possibilities. Being receptive acknowledges that the universe is always trying to teach us things and guide us. Receptivity begins with learning how to listen to your own soul, your own inner source, and al- lowing these insights to enter into your heart and mind. By holding a receptive state of awareness, you harmonize with the vibration of that which is trying to emerge. Your mind and heart can now register the mys- tery and possibilities that are revealed.

When you are receptive, you allow miracles to happen. The truth is that miracles are happening around us all the time, but we don't al- ways notice them because we are not always open to them. We are too caught up in the drama of our life situation and it closes us off from the beauty of meaningful experience. Being receptive allows you to see new possibilities—new ways of being that hadn't occurred to you before.

For Demian and me, being receptive relates directly back to the phone call when we reconnected. Demian had asked me a crucial question:

"Will you forgive me?" If either of us had not been open and recep- tive to a new start, our lives would have continued to drift apart and we wouldn't be here, now, sharing our story with you.

When you are in this open state, your true essence, your true na- ture, will begin to shine through. You will begin to see your Gifts. Clear messages will come to you through multiple means. You may be expe- riencing more coincidences in your life, or suddenly opportunities to share your Gift begin to show up. When you discover your Gift, your life changes. Your self-esteem flourishes because you can feel yourself beginning to live the life you were meant to live. Your newfound joy over who you are creates a vibrational presence. Your energy, commu- nication, compassion, and understanding shift, allowing you to see the world in new ways. Your opportunities have always been there, awaiting your notice.

Opening ourselves to the *possibility of possibility* allowed the two of us to reconnect after so many years apart. It allowed for compassion to emerge and grow. Compassion came from being able to forgive. Receptivity to forgiveness transformed our souls and unlocked new pathways to our Gifts.

Endless Possibilities

Let us define possibility itself. If you take away *every thing* and you are left with *no thing*, then what is possible? *Any thing.* So, it is in this place of "every thing" and "no thing" that we engage possibility. Think of it this way. You have a glass jar that is filled with pennies. By removing all the pennies, you are left with empty space, but in that empty space you can now deposit quarters or flowers or jewelry you craft with your child. The possibilities are limited only by your imagination.

You are undoubtedly curious about the possibilities *Discover the Gift* holds for you, and perhaps you are ready to jump right in. Or perhaps you are still a little reticent to buy into what you may fear is the latest fad. Practicing receptivity at this stage is just a way of opening yourself to the concept that within you is something powerful and life giving, a quality as unique to you as your DNA.

Opening yourself to the possibility of something powerful within you can be a simple step. "Can be" are the key words here. A lot of times we can change our lives simply by becoming aware of what we're thinking about, then thinking about something else. But it's not always that easy. Perhaps you have suffered so much in your life that you doubt whether you were even meant to exist. Let us assure you that we know, without an ounce of doubt, that you (yes, *you*) were created to experience joy, contentment, and a sense of belonging.

This does not imply that discov- ering your Gift is an easy task, but allow yourself to give in a little and let that last sentence resonate within you. It's important to keep in mind that receptivity implies and goes hand in hand with flexibility. It means you are willing to abandon preconditions and expectations about who and what you are. Receptivity is about openness, and flexibility is about being fluid. When you are receptive and fluid, you are able to consider new potentialities around you, able to flow with the vibrational current of the universe.

We have learned that we must not always be set on expecting things to be a certain way. Rather, we know that great Gifts come in unexpected packages.

What comes to you as you become receptive may seem at first mun- dane, or even more than you can handle. But at this stage you do not need to do anything more than acknowledge the thoughts, ideas, and impres- sions that come to you when you're practicing your breathing or reflecting on what you are learning. See them, note them, and let them go. What you notice could be as simple as the sound of windswept leaves, or the stirring of your own spirit in need of your attention. No need to analyze any of this now. Just remember to receive with flexibility. Expect to be confused, excited, disappointed, or even surprised, and know that it is okay. You've only just opened the door to discovering yourself in this way, and it may take a little time before what you find comes together as a whole.

TRANSFORMATIONAL WISDOM

DEMIAN LICHTENSTEIN: To release the shackles around my heart and unchain the extraordinary miracle of my existence, I had to be *open* to the possibility of experiencing my life as a Gift.

SUE MO RTER: For someone who has never contemplated the idea that there is a Gift in their experience, no matter what their experience is— it's a pretty scary place to be!

JACK CANFIELD: Think of it this way: The sun has to shine. It's the nature of the sun to do that. It doesn't withhold its shining. It doesn't shine to get feedback. It shines because that's the sun's nature. Our nature is to love, to express ourselves, to give. Just like nature contains flowers of many different varieties, we're all different varieties of the God con- sciousness manifested in physical form. Knowing that we come from that and that we are returning to that, we can't be anything less than that. We are literally expressions of God.

HIS HOLINESS THE DALAI LAMA: To be harmonious, happier, peace- ful as a community, that's our goal. So in order to achieve that, I think first it is very important to realize that every individual human being has a responsibility to humanity.

MICHAEL BERNARD BECKWITH: If an individual really wants to discover their Gift, they have to ask, "What Gift is trying to emerge and express itself through me? What power is trying to become con- scious of itself as me?" Many people aren't asking that question. They're just asking, "How can I avoid pain? How can I get more stuff? How can I fit into the society in which I'm living? How can I become successful?" Perhaps their model of success is something that has been handed down to them by a high-tech, low-touch consumer-driven society.

Others ask, "How can I become more myself? How can I share my Gifts? How can I activate my potential?" Those are the questions that begin to activate the spiritual faculties within that allow you to hear the inaudible and to see the invisible. By asking these questions you're pull- ing yourself out of the everyday world of mundane questions. Instead you're aware of an interior broadcast that's always being given. We're guided not by the world, but by our hearts. We're guided by our soul's desire to unfold.

NIURKA: Growing up, I remember feeling like I didn't belong on this planet. Like I was an anomaly. I felt so alone, and so disconnected, and so sad. I knew inside that I was destined for more than what was then showing up in my life. I just hadn't trusted it before. Then that escalated into feeling angry, which told me that something had to shift, something had to change. I tuned in to that and realized I had to be receptive, and to ask questions. I began my search from that space. I started asking, "Who am I really? What's my purpose here?" I also noticed that when I asked disempowering questions, like "Why is this happening to me?" I would feel pain. But when I asked higher-vibrational questions, like "What am I grateful for? Who do I love? How can I serve?" then amaz- ing opportunities were revealed.

The quality of our lives is directly proportionate to the qualities of the questions we ask. We create as we speak.

STE WA RT EME RY: The dictionary says that consciousness means to be aware of what we are doing and why. If you're not aware, you can't make choices. To make choices you have to accept that you *have* choices or you can't make them.

JACK CANFIELD: What most of us do, unfortunately, because we are educated by our parents, by school, by the military, is we lose touch with that essence, that questioning. And then we end up at the top of the lad- der fifty years later only to discover that the ladder is leaning up against the wrong wall. Then we think we've wasted our lives. Not to discover your Gift is to die with the music still inside of you.

The first step is to take the time to explore inside you and discover your passion. Do whatever's necessary to keep it alive. By doing that you will naturally bring to the world what it needs. Now, it might take years to master that, to bring it forward in a way that fulfills you, but have the courage to set goals, to ask for what you want, to risk rejection, to perse- vere in the face of obstacles.

MARK VICTOR HANSEN: What's my Gift? What's my Gift? What's my Gift? What's my Gift? You've got to go to bed with this question every night. You have to contemplate, ruminate, and meditate on it. Say it before you close your eyes and turn out the light: "What's my Gift? What's my Gift? What's my Gift? What's my Gift?" You will wake up with the answer. Your subconscious *must* answer. It is robotic in nature, so if you put the question in as a mantra, the answer is going to start bouncing back.

Here's what you'll discover: not one Gift but a multiplicity of Gifts. And they work together for the greater good of your becoming a self-actualized, fully functioning, no-limit self-master.

When your Gift starts to unfold, you are unstoppable. You are immensely powerful. You knew this as a child, and now you've got to re-remember it because we get amnesia as we get older. So, go out today and create your tomorrows so that you are financially free and indepen- dent, so that you're free to go and do what you're supposed to do before someone tells you that you have to go to work. Use your inspired, divine, magnificent creativity to make a difference.

CYNTHIA M. RUIZ: The key reason for discovering your Gift is for happiness. All of us really want to be happy. I think what we need to do is look at ourselves in the mirror and ask, "What percentage of the time am I happy and what percentage of the time am I not?" If you are not happy most of the time, then you need to change your life. Living mo- ment to moment can help you really achieve happiness.

The other key is being grateful. We have so much to be grateful for. Every day, when I wake up, I make my gratitude list—a list of what I'm grateful for. Having that vibration of gratitude first thing in the morn- ing really helps me be and stay happy for the entire day. The happier I am, the more people act and react to me in joyful ways.

JANET BR AY ATTWOOD: To help find my Gift I had people tell me what I was great at. I once heard a seminar speaker refer to a survey that had been done with the hundred most successful people in the United States. The results showed that all these successful people were living what they considered their top five passions. At the time, I was strug- gling at my job, not making enough money. I couldn't stand getting out of bed. When I heard about the survey, I got a jolt from the universe: *Smack! Wham!* If I could just figure out what my top five passions were, I'd be just like those hundred most successful people in the United States. It's not a mistake that you love what you love. The universe doesn't play tricks.

DAVID "AVOCADO" WOLFE: You've got to look into your life and ask, "What would I do no matter what? If the world blew up, what would I do anyway? If I lost my family, what would I do every day for free? What would I do without any remuneration? What would I do as a non- profit charity?" If you ask yourself those questions enough, and particu- larly if you meditate on them, I believe it's inevitable that you will find your Gift.

PERSONAL PRACTICES

SHEILA R. MC KEITHEN: Practice more solitude. Many people are afraid to be alone with themselves. But it is in the silence of your own soul that your inner voice speaks and you're able to hear and follow the voice as it directs you.

You can also practice loving yourself. Give yourself permission to live your dreams, to be well. Give yourself permission to be forgiven for past mistakes. Give yourself permission to start over. All of these are acts of love.

LUCIA DE GARCIA: Go into the woods. Bathe yourself in a stream. Lis- ten to the birds singing. Go to the ocean and listen to the music of the waves. The world, the universe, is talking to you.

GROWTH OPPO RTUNITIES

Growth Opportunities are simple exercises to guide you along a path of self-discovery. These opportunities are meant to be both enjoyable and serious, fun and accessible. Some tasks will specifically require you to write in a journal. We encourage you to have a journal, some- thing in which you can take notes, write, draw, doodle. This journal should be just for this process. It is your "discovery journal," and it is meant to be used now as much as in the future, to chronicle and remind you of the ideas and inspirations that came to you during this process.

Becoming Present to Your Breath

We spoke earlier about breathing, and the exercise that follows builds on that. It may seem rudimentary, even for new practitioners, but it is none- theless effective and rewarding. We need to breathe to live, and when we direct our breath, we are, in essence, directing our lives.

The important part of this exercise is to be aware of your breath and your posture. You may lie on the floor (with some padding), on your back, head on the floor, legs extended straight out, hands by your sides. If you have a sensitive back or injuries, lie with your legs bent at the knees, or however you are most comfortable. You may also do this exercise while standing, and as you become most comfortable with the exercise, you can practice it sitting or walking. Always be mindful to keep good posture, as poor posture restricts your breath flow and takes your attention away from your breathing.

Close your eyes if that works for you—if not, keep them open— and observe your breath without consciously trying to change it. Take a deep breath. Focus on each breath in and each breath out. Notice the natural movement of the breath. As you watch your breath, other thoughts or sensations will inevitably come into your consciousness. This is natural and normal. Just acknowledge them all without dwelling on them . . . and let them pass.

Breathe. Everything in your existence is breath. Relax into the infinite being you are and know that you are alive. Feel into the depth of who and what you already are. Pure energy, pure light, pure being at play in the universe, following a path to the realization and discovery of the Gift that you already are and always have been. Breathe. Simply because it's the one thing you cannot live without. A human being can and will endure hardships beyond comprehension, but the one thing we can only endure for a few moments is lack of breath. So breathe.

4 X 4 Breath Practice

Find a quiet and comfortable place to perform this exercise. You can sit or lie down, whatever is best for you. Whatever position you take, try to keep your back straight.

Now please take four deep breaths.

1. Count to four as you inhale through the nose.
2. Count to four as you hold the breath.
3. Count to four while you exhale through your mouth.
4. Count to four as you hold your breath. Repeat.

Do this exercise a total of four times. How do you feel? Calmer? Re- laxed? Empowered? Frustrated? Foolish? Disappointed?

Just remember that you don't have to think about accomplishing any- thing with this exercise. It's just a good practice to use anytime to be- come aware of the present moment and to bring calm to your body and mind. You'll be able to use this simple practice anytime to relax, focus, and reconnect with yourself. The most important fact to know about breath is that it brings oxygen to all parts of our bodies and increases our awareness of ourselves and the world around us.

Mirror Practice

For this next practice you will need a mirror, a pen, and your discovery journal. You can do this practice standing or sitting. This activity is de- signed to help you see new and wonderful aspects about yourself and what is possible for you.

You will need at least 20 private minutes without distractions. We strongly recommend doing this exercise as you begin your journey, as it will help open up possibilities you may never have thought of before but that you are now ready to hear.

Remember to breathe and to hold good posture, as this allows oxygen to enter all areas of your body and mind.

Find your favorite mirror and settle comfortably in front of it. Re- member receptivity and flexibility as you begin, because looking in a mir- ror is something we all probably do many times a day. But now we'd like you to try seeing yourself with new eyes. What do you think you'll see?

———————

As you look in the mirror, ask yourself the following questions:

- What do I like about myself most?
- What wonderful part of myself have I not given credence to before now?
- Do I want a life of joy and fulfillment?
- Do I want to be happy?
- What percentage of the time am I happy?
- What percentage of the time do I want to be happy?

If happiness is feeling good about who I am and who I choose to be, what am I willing to do to be happy?

- What is standing in my way right now, preventing me from moving forward and realizing a fuller life?
- What talents, qualities, and Gifts seek to express them- selves through me?
- What am I reaching for that will help me on my path?

Allow yourself time to answer these questions. Listen to what your inner guidance is saying, just listen and don't worry about the "how can I accomplish this?" of any possibility that arises. Allow all possibilities to exist. Take time to write down all thoughts, feelings, visions, and the like in your discovery journal.

———————

As you read through the rest of this book, take time at the end of each chapter to journal some reflections on where you are on this journey. These reflections don't have to be anything more than impressions—your journal is just a tool for you. It's not for others to see. Think about con- cepts that may seem difficult to you; write about anything that pops into your head and your heart. Everything comes up for a reason. Your vision for yourself is the most powerful tool you have.

STEP 2: INTENTION

Orange Mandala
Intention and Attention = Orange Lotus Sparkles

•　　•　　•

Keep your thoughts positive because your thoughts become your words. Keep your words positive because your words become your behaviors.

— GANDHI

As we've seen, Step 1 is about being open to a new journey that leads to deeper self-discovery, self-understanding, and expression of who you really are.

Step 2, intention, is the act of setting a new purpose for your life— a new goal—inspired by your receptivity. Intention is an act of dec- laration, an act of decision, an act of will. Intention means setting yourself free of limiting patterns, habits, and beliefs so that you can create a life-affirming system of thinking and living in alignment with your new purpose.

Manifesting Intention

It is through being attentive to your intention, to your creative thoughts, to what you are thinking about and focusing on, that you manifest and cocreate your life. Intention works by first setting a destination, and then feeling that you have already arrived. This simple action invokes the cre- ative and imaginative energy of the universe, which helps you unlock your Gift.

When we think about something, we typically put it off into the future with thoughts like "One day I hope, maybe if only I wish it, it could be, but it isn't, so I'll just hang around and pray for it." Instead, think (intend) from that future now. Do not think *about* it but rather think *from* it.

How do you think and feel from a future state? Go back to Step 1, receptivity. What did you think and feel when you were receptive and open to possibilities? Meditate on the vision and feelings that inspired you. This is a future state. Then use your breathing exercises while you focus your mind on that vision. Use your imagination to hold yourself in that space. This is the essence of intention.

Here's another way to focus on your intention. Start by taking four deep breaths (see the "4 X 4 Breath Practice" on page 89). Relax. Now, as you're breathing, put your attention on your intention. As your atten- tion expands, so will the power of your intention. Intend that your imag- ination will reveal its secrets to you, and intend that you have already lived a life of grace, fulfillment, gratitude, and love. Use your imagina- tion to create a picture of the end result. Frame it and focus. Make your intention colorful. Give the picture sound. Add music. Make the picture move. Give it a sweet smell. Now reach out and touch it. Feel it. Taste it. It is yours.

This is the secret of manifesting intention.

TRANSFORMATIONAL WISDOM

SHAJEN JOY AZIZ: The best way to begin a journey of discovery is to focus your newly receptive mind on what you want and to ask questions like "Who am I? What lights me up and inspires me? What is my Gift? How can I serve? How can I share my purpose?"

BILL HARRIS: Your mind creates everything that happens to you. What happens looks like it's created by something *out there,* but it isn't; it's being created inside your head. What you decide to pay attention to has a huge effect on what happens to you, on what you create in your life. What most people don't get is that what you pay attention to is a choice.

CHERIF AZIZ: One of my passions has always been movies, and when I went to the University of Vermont, I entered their film program. It wasn't the strongest school for film, and at the time, I was overcome with fear because I kept reading about all these people who go into the indus- try and fail. It seems that everybody on the planet wants to be associated with movies, but there are so many actors, producers, and directors who don't make it in the business. Unfortunately, I let my fears rule me, and I ended up switching majors.

Years later, I had become a successful entrepreneur. I was really good at selling, but deep down, I felt regret for not having followed my dream. Since embracing my Gift with Shajen and Demian and becoming a core member of the Discover the Gift team, I am living the dream I have always wanted to pursue. Sure, there was fear along the way, but now I live by a very simple motto: "Don't be afraid." This is the secret to intention—be fearless.

SUE MO RTER: There have been many conversations in recent years about the idea that what you focus on, you attract. The idea that what happens in your life is based on what you think about is absolutely true. When we think about something, a certain related energy is created, not only in our bodies but in our personal space, our reality. Then that real- ity unfolds.

MARK VICTOR HANSEN: What you think about comes about, right? If you want to know who you are going to be five minutes from now, or five years from now, tell me what your dominant thought forms are and I'll tell you where you're moving to or how you're staying stagnant.

BILL HARRIS: Most people don't direct their minds in an intentional way. They run on autopilot. Most people whose lives aren't working are still unconsciously and unintentionally thinking it into being. But be- cause they don't see the connection, they continue to dislike the results.

BOBBI DEPO RTER: We sabotage ourselves a lot with negative think- ing. When people feel anger or are depressed, it's usually because they're thinking about something in the past—something they have no control over. Only when you are in the present do you have control over your thoughts, your actions, how you're feeling. When you're feeling negative, you're only doing it to yourself in the present.

SONIA POWERS: A lot of people live their entire lives at the effect of everything around them. They don't see their life as something that they can make happen. They see their life as something that happens to them.

HIS HOLINESS SRI SRI R AVI SHANKAR: When you want to discover the Gift that nature has given to you, the first thing is that we must stop blaming ourselves. Self-blame is the biggest obstruction in recognizing one's Gift.

JANET BR AY ATTWOOD: Self-blame will stop you every time from being able to live the life you were meant to live. Thoughts like "I'm not beautiful enough. I'm not smart enough. I'm not rich enough. I'm not educated enough. I'm not the right color." When you let these things take over and drive your life, they do.

LYNN POMPEI: I wanted to be accomplished, and I wanted to be suc- cessful. Although I kept it secret, I also really wanted to get married and be a mother. But I thought I couldn't have that life and my career too. I thought I'd have to choose one or the other. I was conflicted, and as a result I felt paralyzed. And then I realized that every moment is a Gift, and that's why it's called "the present." I realized that everything I wanted was right in front of me. So I focused my intention on what I wanted and gave myself permission to choose both.

HIS HOLINESS SRI SRI R AVI SHANKAR: You know, the very inter- esting thing about our mind is that when our mind is calm and col- lected and it's focused, it gets enormous energy, enormous power, and can manifest its own intentions.

HIS HOLINESS THE DALAI LAMA: The ultimate creator is the human mind or consciousness. It immediately creates an atmosphere: sometimes pleasant, sometimes unpleasant. Then this energy, it creates a chain re- action on two levels, one with immediate effect, one with a long-term effect. So you see, in order to change the external thing, we must first change the routine within ourselves.

JACK CANFIELD: In order to change reactive thought into proactive thought, you first have to become aware of your thoughts. Watch your thoughts, and you'll notice that all day long they just come and come and come. As you're watching, you begin to see the fear and the doubts and the judgments. And then you realize that just because you can *observe* your thoughts, *you are not your thoughts.*

Once you get to that place of *"I have a mind, but I'm not my mind. I have an intellect, but I'm not my intellect,"* you see that you are actually a pure center of awareness and choice. You can choose the thoughts that will take you where you want to go. You can choose the thoughts that will support your dreams, that will uplift you and your family—and humanity. That's when you become intentional with your thoughts.

JANET BRAY ATTWOOD: There's a cool study, the Bowling Study, in which two pairs of bowlers were told to study videos of themselves bowling. One pair was told to study all the things they did wrong; the other pair was told to study all the things they did right. Which one of the teams improved the most afterward?

The team that studied what they did right.

What you focus your attention on grows stronger in your life. Every single moment is a choice. Where do you want to put your attention?

You're the cocreator of your universe. It's up to you! How do you want your world to be? Make that choice.

JACK CANFIELD: It takes time to undo and release the conditioning you've been given. It's not an overnight process. Research shows it takes thirty days of uninterrupted discipline to get a new habit into your life. That can be a new paradigm you believe in, a new habit of thinking, a new habit of behavior—like flossing your teeth. And if you hold this new thought, if you do whatever is necessary to make it stick, you re- claim the essence of who you are and release all the negative blocks that have taken over for years. Then you naturally step into who you are, you naturally express your Gift. This is not hard, this is easy.

DEMIAN LICHTENSTEIN: In the process of reconnecting with my sister, a veil had been lifted. I could see that the "choices" I had made in my life were not really choices, but reactions. I had never *really* chosen my life. I had been living out of alignment with the spiritual laws of the uni- verse. I had to decide on my intentions and then focus and connect with them. I realized that I wasn't my past (a very arrogant and self-centered and righteous ass); I was an emerging possibility. My life was headed in an entirely new direction.

It's said that in the darkness of night, one candle can be seen from miles away. It was time for me to light my own candle. I did that in part by seeking out people and places that could coach me onto a higher level of understanding so I could be conscious and more present to the Gifts available to me in every moment, every waking hour. I also began to breathe more. I've been breathing a lot more. Breathe.

B ARBARA DE ANGELIS: A lot of us discount what we have to offer because we can't see how it's going to make us money, or it's not going to make us famous, or we're not going to get invited to be on *Oprah*. So we believe we are not making a difference. But making a difference is really about the way you show up in the world every day. In fact, know it or not, like it or not, you're already making a difference just by your pres- ence. It may be a good difference or a bad difference, a large difference or a small difference, but you had an effect on everyone who saw you, felt you, or heard you today. So the question is not whether you can make a difference, but what kind of difference are you making?

SHEILA R. MC KEITHEN: If people looked for their Gift, they would find it. But the world has mesmerized each of us to some degree. The world says the power is in status symbols. The power is in the position you hold in the world. The power is in what kind of automobile you drive, what kind of neighborhood you live in. The power is in the money. In truth, the power is in you. You can get all those things if that's what you consciously choose. But there are also infinite other choices that come from your Gift, which has always been there. But you'll never find it if your eyes are stuck on someone else's Gift. Your intention is all about focusing on yourself and your own dreams and consciously in- tending to activate the Gifts in yourself to make your dreams come true.

PERSONAL PRACTICES

LUCIA DE GARCIA AND SHAJEN JOY AZIZ: Secure a day, or half a day, during which you can be alone in order to reconnect with yourself. Whether it's a day at the spa, a bike ride through your favorite park, a long drive on your favorite road to your most cherished place, a visit to a museum or a botanical garden, whatever it is, it is perfect as long as you do it alone.

During your time of solitude, notice all things that come up for you, good, bad, exciting, or sad. Most important, write down any thoughts, words, and issues that come up along the way in your journal. Do not hold on to any of the negative feelings or emotions. Allow them to be noticed and let go. Be constantly mindful of your presence—how you are feeling, what you are thinking, and how you show up in each mo- ment. What kind of presence do you need to be for the world around you to respond in positive ways?

JACK CANFIELD: I spent a year wearing a rubber band around my left wrist. I call it snap practice. Every time I became aware of having a negative thought I would snap the band. It wasn't to punish myself, but simply to heighten and reinforce my awareness. I also had friends who made themselves part of my "team." If I said something negative, they'd point it out immediately. If I said, "We can't get it done," or "That guy's an idiot," they'd say, "Snap yourself!" So I'd snap and then I'd rephrase it. "You know, that guy is acting in a way that doesn't match my criteria of how I think someone should act." Or, "We can get it done—we're just going to have to hire three more people to get it done." It took me about six months to turn myself around consistently.

MARK VICTOR HANSEN: Every one of us can raise his or her self- worth internally and spiritually by decorating our "home entertainment center," called the mind, in an eyes-closed visualization processes. See yourself as you want to be, not as who you are.

You've got to come from the space of full utilization of your Gift. The operative preposition is *from*. You've got to *be* there before you *get* there.

When I visualize, I go inside my secret place, I see myself on a stage of my imagination. I see myself as strong, healthy, happy—a radiant soul, exuding self-confidence. I see myself speaking before wondrous audiences who are really getting it. I experience my words turning on their inner lights and getting the results. I see myself in the media saying exactly what needs to be said to the audience. I see people going out and buying the books, or whatever I'm selling.

If you do this kind of interior visualization, which can run from a few seconds to a few minutes, and start from the end result, you'll start catching up to it with amazing success, because it has to happen *inside* before it can happen outside. What you *impress* is what you always *express*.

GROWTH OPPORTUNITIES

"Being Right" Practice

In your journal, write down the names of four people you feel the need to be right about. Now take a moment and identify *what* you feel you need to be right about. Now ask yourself, "If I gave up being right and making them wrong, what would be possible? What Gift might I discover?"

Many of us are addicted to being right. Is it because it makes us feel superior to—or better than—someone else? Does it let us off the hook for not being responsible for the cocreation of our own existence? What- ever the reason, the need to always be right can destroy your life. It nearly destroyed ours. We can tell you for sure that *Discover the Gift* would not exist if the two of us had not given up being right. From there, forgive- ness and healing could begin.

Now we encourage you to call those who are important to you and share and acknowledge what you discovered when you gave up being right. Express what possibilities show up for you in relationship to each person. Maybe nothing grand will come of it, or maybe, just maybe, an incredible connection will occur with someone you love, and an entire world will unfold because of your courage and honesty.

Awareness Meditation

The goal of this meditation is to bring your attention to your body and to become present to what you are experiencing at this moment. Lie, sit, or stand quietly. Close your eyes and notice if there are any thoughts or sensations in any part of you. Most of the time you will have some sensation somewhere: your lower back, your palms, your shoulders, your knees. The sensation can be anything, even one barely noticed. It could be pleasant or unpleasant; it doesn't really matter. Be aware of yourself. Focus closely on every little feeling you are having. Don't try to force yourself to focus, just notice the sensations, your thoughts and feelings. Just let your attention rest on this present moment. If your mind drifts, take a deep breath and slowly bring your attention back to the sensation. Become present to its presence inside you.

Are you feeling relaxed or tense? What needs your attention? Listen to your source. What are the messages coming through?

After this practice, take a few moments with your journal to jot down ideas, feelings, sensations, recurring themes, and the like. Allow all aspects that come up for you to be valid for that moment. Don't edit yourself in your journal. Take the time later to look back through your journal to re- mind yourself of what came up at other times. In fact, reading an uncen- sored account of your experiences at a later date can be a Gift all in itself.

4 X 4 Breath Practice, Part 2

Let's take another moment to pause and become present in this moment, to our breath, and to our bodies. Do the 4 X 4 Breath Practice given on page 89 in this way:

1. Breathe in receptivity and breathe out any obstacles in your way.
2. Breathe in flexibility and breathe out rigidity.

3. Breathe in your intentions with the journey you are taking. When you exhale, breathe out any and all feel-ings that block your intentions. Get rid of the worry about *how*.

4. Breathe in attention, and focus on what makes you happy. Hold your breath for an extra moment, feeling the es-sence of your life force. Hold it . . . hold it . . . and now, let it go. Feel how alive you are in this moment. Notice your mind, your body, and your emotions. Write down or draw any of the feelings, sensations, or thoughts in your journal. This is presence to your presence.

The more you become aware of your thoughts, the more you begin to notice that you are not your thoughts and that you can actually con-trol your thoughts. This is where intention is so important. Your inten-tion activates your path. When you place your attention on what makes you happy, on what you love, and what inspires you, those things are amplified. As Terry Tillman says, "Where you look is where you go." So when you can hold your focus on what you intend, the pathway to reach that goal begins to reveal itself.

All negative thoughts have to go. There's no room for them. Our friend Scott Petersen puts it this way: "Always give energy to the things you love, and always take energy away from the things you don't love." As you strengthen your ability to hold your focus on the Gifts that reveal themselves to you, those Gifts arrive in your life faster and faster. When you connect with your Gifts, it starts a fire in your heart and your pas-sions explode.

STEP 3: ACTIVATION

Yellow Mandala
Inner-Action and Inter-Action = Yellow Lotus Sparkles

•   •   •

First have a blueprint in mind, then implement.

— HIS HOLINESS THE DALAI LAMA

What you leave out of the frame is just as important as what you include in the frame.

— FONDA JOY SEGAL

We have to take action in the same way we have to exercise. We can only learn by doing. Whatever Gifts you have, they're going to require some effort, some discipline, some study. I've had to work fairly hard to develop my talents, and that's true for everybody in any trade or profession. We watch Fred Astaire dance, and it looks effortless, but he worked for hours every day to make it look that way. It takes time and action to master your skill, and I think it's a crime when you don't. Our strengths, our qualities, our character come from being committed to the development of whatever it is we have so we can become a true master.

—JACK CANFIELD

Activation is the step at which you build on your receptivity and intention by actively engaging in the work of personal growth and development.

You may find that you are passionate about your new intention, but your thoughts and emotions are mostly from your past, from the old you, and may now be holding you back. You will have to actively recondi- tion them, working toward your true potential. It is not always easy to change former ways of being. Your personal thought patterns and inter- nal beliefs have had many years to build strong roots and are not always willing to be uprooted easily. The most important thing you can do at this step is take specific actions to develop yourself and your Gift. It's time to take the step and put your energy into what you love.

Activation has an inner component and an outer component, which we have termed *inner-action* and *inter-action*. You will not only have to en- gage with yourself in this work, but also with everyone and everything else. Since action must be applied in order for us to manifest things on earth, we must therefore engage in actions that support our inner thoughts, emotions, and desires. Not to mention, we must continuously choose our intentions and words wisely.

Moving from Intention to Activation

As you have gathered, this activation can't be meaningful without your having taken the previous two steps of receptivity and intention. When you have clear intention, you can transmute negative energy into power- ful positive actions that build a foundation of self-esteem and trust in your own self-expression and leadership. Any action is better than no action, because even a mistake will guide you. If you are aware and taking action in the direction of your own Gift, you can discover the fulfillment of your purpose and reason for being.

In short, activation is about taking action.

You can think and read and plan and talk all you want, but if you don't get out there and convert your intention into action, your desires can never be attained. For instance, the law of attraction cannot attract what you desire until you have actively reconditioned your mind and emotions and are willing to put your energy into what you want to bring into your life. Our brains are large muscles, and the more we use them toward specific goals, the stronger they become and the more possibility we create to attract what we want.

There are two sets of actions that will help activate our Gift. The first, *inner-action,* is about working with your self and implementing your understanding of intention. It means going inside, spending time with your source, and listening. This is the private side of activation.

Inter-action, the public side of activation, means engaging, interacting, and participating with yourself and others and allowing your potential Gift to unfold. By doing so, you are supporting your thoughts, dreams, and emotions through your actions and your language.

TRANSFORMATIONAL WISDOM

JANET BRAY ATTWOOD: Take action, and choose in favor of your passion. Choose in favor of the things that have the greatest meaning to you. Your passions are like bread crumbs that lead you onto the path of your Gift. Just know that every moment is a choice, and you're either choosing to be closer to your Gift or moving farther away. So what do you want to choose?

SHAJEN JOY AZIZ: When I realized teaching and educating was a major aspect of my purpose, I had to come to terms with my calling. This for me meant that I had to return to school, and all my old thoughts and feelings about myself and my failures at school came rushing back into my being. Suddenly I was faced with every obstacle and every possible reason I did not need to listen to this inner knowing, this calling.

DEMIAN LICHTENSTEIN: Activation necessitates focus and clar- ity. As my mother said when she began to teach me photography, "You should be clear about your intention. What do you want to say with that picture? What are you focusing on?" Focus is the critical issue in dealing with pictures, and it's interesting how easily that concept crosses over into everyday life. That which you focus on increases; that which you focus on brings clarity; that which gets your attention becomes manifest through your actions.

I could either continue to suffer by constantly re-creating a past of pain, sorrow, and blame, or I could embrace an unknown future with power, courage, freedom to choose, and an infinite realm of possibility at my fingertips. This book and movie are just an expression of that choice.

I was in Rome and on the phone with my sister, Shajen. What she said was profound: "When is the work you're doing in the world going to match the man I know? When's that going to happen? I know you're really good at blowing things up, and that it's a lot of fun, but frankly it's not a match for who you've become."

That was a great question and a greater insight. I really had to think about it. I realized that even though I was focused on making big movies, I was also trying so hard to get to the next biggest thing I could do.

Suddenly I had my answer right in front of me. It had been there the entire time. My purpose was now clear: to share everything I'd learned, and all the amazing people I'd met on my journey, with the rest of the world.

And I'm just one of many experiencing this awakening, this rise in consciousness.

I can assure you of one thing: transformation isn't usually pretty. For me it was filled with tears, frustration, and losing an identity I had become deeply attached to. But I wouldn't trade the Gifts I got out of it for the world.

HIS HOLINESS THE DALAI LAMA: The future, good or bad, entirely depends upon present action.

STE WA RT EME RY: The secret of life is finding out what you love to do, actively developing a deliberate practice, and getting really good at it. That's the foundation that will lead you on a serendipitous journey to riches beyond your wildest imagination.

RICK MARS: Forget the word "can't." I've talked with people around the world, and one thing that comes up again and again is this word. "I *can't* seem to find it. I *can't* do it. I *can't* get there. I *can't* this, I *can't* that." I would like to share a little secret. When you were a little kid, there was no such thing as *can't*—which is not the same as being told not to climb so high or not to touch the hot stove. Those are different. Instead of saying you can't, take a step. It might not be the right step, but you won't know unless you do it. In order to find your Gift, you need to take ac- tion. Move forward. If it doesn't feel like love or it's not working toward love, you're probably on the wrong path anyway.

SIR KEN ROBINSON: If you're doing something with which you don't resonate properly, five minutes can feel like an hour. But if you're doing the thing that is part of your being, that emanates from you, then an hour can feel like five minutes.

MA RY MANIN MORRISSEY: Each person is as unique as their thumb- print. You'll begin to become present to your uniqueness and get a clue to your Gift by paying attention to what you love, and then ac- tively choosing it. You'll notice that when you are in your Gift, you feel more alive, you feel more passionate, you feel as if you were born for this.

PENNEY PEIRCE: When you discover your Gift, you don't have to make yourself happy—you'll just *be* happy. You feel trusting. You feel the voice of your soul come through as it reveals your path to you. It brings you what you need. It connects you with everyone you need.

DAVID "AVOCADO" WOLFE: As you activate your Gift in the world, you get momentum behind you. And there is no maximum level, because the Gift is scalable. You keep touching more people, and that cranks up the momentum and inspirational power.

SHAJEN JOY AZIZ: You must align your Gifts with action. When you do, the possibilities are endless. The mere act of speaking out loud creates ripples in the atmosphere and thus begins the journey of the thought, because it has been made into tangible energy. Aligning think- ing and action with your Gifts unlocks potentiality, and sharing your Gifts also creates possibility for others. There are multiple layers and dimensions to our Gifts, our talents, and our inspiration. When we truly share who we are and what lights us up, we empower all to do the same.

DEMIAN LICHTENSTEIN: Although filmmaking was my passion, it turned out to be a stepping-stone to discovering an even bigger Gift: to first and foremost become a spiritual and compassionate human. To acti- vate that Gift, I had to begin to heal the relationships within my family. This meant opening myself to love, and to the risk I'd so long avoided of being disappointed, abandoned, and hurt.

CHRISTINE STEVENS: When we take action, we have to follow what feels naturally joyful and remove the internal critic that whispers, "I'm not good enough." You have to let that go. For me, the drum is a great tool for releasing, because without words, through energy, you can say anything that you need to say, then let it go, and create more space for the creative force.

I first noticed the drumbeat coming from a room as I walked down a hallway. It pulled me in, and I stayed for hours that felt like minutes. There were no notes to read, there was no orchestra director to follow; everybody played off of one another's energy. I could let go of so much of what I thought I knew about music. I didn't have to think. It's a great metaphor for a beautiful way to live, to really listen, to harmonize, to collaborate, and to free our spirit.

Just like the drum, you have to let go and stop thinking and just fall into the groove, the greater vibration that you are.

JOE VI TALE: A lot of people lie to themselves about what they'd really like to do. They get stuck.

To recover from that, there are steps you can take. The first is to face your fears and be honest with yourself. The second is to ask yourself what you liked to do as a child. The third is to pretend you've won the lottery and you already went around the globe seven times, you bought fifteen cars, you have seven houses, and you've had more dessert than ever. Now that you've done all that, what do you want to do next? That's probably your calling. For me, following my passion is what keeps the fire alive. Even if I don't know where it's going or if I'll make any money. We each have a piece of the puzzle to contribute to life. Years ago I gave a talk to a small group in Houston. I walked in with a jigsaw puzzle, and I gave everybody in the room a piece. Then I said, "Look at the piece." They did, but it made no sense, and it certainly didn't suggest the whole picture. That's how it seems when you look at your own calling.

You don't know what it means in terms of everything. But when we all put our pieces together . . . the whole world takes shape.

People know what they love to do, but they've talked themselves out of it because to follow that passion means they have to take responsibil- ity for it. They have to confront why they waited so long, and all the rest. So most of us just settle for lying to ourselves and saying, "I don't know what I want to do with my life. I don't know what my hobbies are. I don't know what my interests are."

That's bull. We always know. We just have to get over our fear of tak- ing action.

B ARBARA DE ANGELIS: Once I watched a diamond cutter take a raw diamond and cut and shape it. If you've never seen a raw diamond, it doesn't look like much. But as he carved and chipped and shaped, all of a sudden this light began to emerge. It came from the middle of the diamond, but you couldn't see it until the stone was cracked, cut, and shaped.

SUE MO RTER: I was a member of several spiritual communities as a young adult and deep into a soulful, earnest exploration of "What's life all about?" and "Who am I in this life experience?" Then I realized that some of the teachers I knew were not practicing ethically. I had to make a decision. I had to take action. I decided to leave. As a result, my entire world collapsed. My friends weren't allowed to speak to me. I kept questioning myself. But I also realized that the only thing we can really trust is our inner wisdom, our gut feeling. When we act upon that, new worlds open. We may do the wrong thing for ourselves, or the right, but we learn from experience, our actions are now intentional, and we are on the path, not watching from the side of the road.

By leaving my community and going through the strife, I found a strength within myself that I was able to trust—and the ability to bring that forward. Out of that, tremendous opportunities began to unfold.

PERSONAL PRACTICES

BILL HARRIS: Whatever your mind can conceive and believe, it can achieve. Once you focus on what you want and are willing to take action, the world starts to unfold for you. That creates a bit of experience, as well as the belief that by focusing your mind and taking appropriate ac- tion, learning from the action and continuing to take more action, there's a whole pile of evidence that yes, indeed, you can do anything.

I'm talking about taking yourself from automatic to intentional. So decide on something you want. Declare your intention. As you focus and prepare for action, you begin to notice resources in your environ- ment that you didn't notice before because you were filtering them out by thinking of something else. You can use these resources to take action and move toward getting the goal. You also begin to develop the internal resources you might need to achieve your goal.

Here are four ways taking action will work for you:

1. You get ideas.
2. You notice resources.
3. You develop internal qualities you need.
4. You become motivated.

So take action. Sometimes it works out exactly the way you wanted. Sometimes not. However, in the latter case, you learn valuable lessons. There are really only two things that can happen when you take action: either (1) you get what you want, or (2) you learn something new. The idea is to take action and then evaluate what happened. Based on what you learned, which could be either "I want to do more of this, because it worked," or "That didn't quite work, so how can I tweak it so it works better?" you take action again. Then you evaluate again. Then you take more action. And then you just keep doing that, always focusing on where you want to go, until you get there.

DAVID "AVOCADO" WOLFE: Before you react, hesitate. Before you act and react, hesitate. Before I eat anything, I say a prayer. This moment of hesitation is a really great habit to adopt. We've all had the experience of going through half a bag of chips before we realize what happened. The hesitation allows the compassion to come in so that I'm allowing myself to calm down and make intelligent choices.

JACK CANFIELD: Be real. Say what's going on for you. Communication is served when you're authentically being yourself. I have a phrase in my seminars: "Tell the truth faster." So many of us do not communicate au- thentically. Instead, we want to manipulate and affect the other person. When we do that, we don't have a connection at the heart level. But by being honest and just bringing forward whatever we're passionate about, whatever we're feeling, whatever we want to say, whatever we want to contribute to life, we get honest and true communication. I think that's critical. Share honest feedback, even if it's anger. It might be the thing really needed, even if it's uncomfortable. Authenticity can lead to real healing and growth.

MARY MANIN MORRISSEY: There's a moment when you take action and let go of what has been your life before, of what you've known be- fore. If you're facing a big issue, it's easy to get discouraged. It's easy to feel like, "Ugh! It's bigger than me." So having some kind of spiritual practice that's yours, no matter what it is—find the one that works for you—keeps you in touch with that part of you that is actually bigger than the problems you have.

For instance: I have the honor of having eight grandchildren, seven of whom are young. I've learned something from them as I've watched them all learn to walk these past few years. They would be crawling along, but they would all get pulled by a longing because they'd see their older sib- lings or parents walking on their legs. And they'd go, "I want that, too!" And so they'd learn to pull themselves up and hang on.

Sometimes we hang on to old ways that have worked for us in the past. And yet we know we'd love to create something new and make a difference. If you follow that longing, then ultimately there's a moment in which you let go of what seems sturdy and go for it. Finally you're willing to traverse the gap between what's known and what's next.

At first, while learning new skills, you're unstable, you're insecure. You might fall down like young ones learning to walk. But you can't go back, and so eventually you'll pull yourself up again, take tiny steps, get a little farther, and then, miraculously, walk.

It always happens. How do I know? I never saw one of those children fall down the umpteenth time and go, "That's it. I give up. I'm just not meant to be a walker."

Uh-uh. They went back and did it again.

GROWTH OPPO RTUNITIES

Unfolding the Gift Exercise

1. Write down the names of the eight most important people in your life, and describe what you think is most extraordinary about them.
2. Now ask the eight most important people in your life to tell you what your Gifts are, and write them down.
3. Take time to reflect on what these people tell you your Gifts are. Notice whether there is a common theme. Write down your thoughts, feelings, and "aha" moments.
4. Now sit back, take a deep breath, close your eyes, and ask yourself, "What Gift inside of me wants to come out?" Allow any and all thoughts to be valid. Notice the ideas "downloading" and the feelings you have about those ideas. Let the strongest visions come to the top. Then open your eyes and write down any and all thoughts, actions, and desires that come to mind.

For the next few days, be aware of this practice, and no- tice in your daily life where there are opportunities for your Gift to emerge. When you notice the thoughts, ac- tions, and desires, write them down and visualize them. Focus on what makes you happy, joyous, and inspired. What Gifts are happening all around you? What do you notice?

Golden Beam Meditation

This meditation is a simple method of transforming your energy. You should practice this Golden Beam Meditation process at least a couple of times a week. The best time to practice it is early in the morning just before you get out of bed. Begin the exercise as soon as you wake, the reason being that when you are coming out of sleep, you are very fresh—you haven't started your laundry list yet and clouded your mind with thoughts of your day ahead.

Stay in your bed, lying on your back with your hands by your side, and keep your eyes closed. When you breathe in, visualize a great golden beam of light entering through your head and into your body. Visualize the light penetrating through your head deep into your being and then going out through your toes. Imagine the golden light spiraling through every cell in your body, cleansing and renewing as it sweeps through and out. Keep your breath slow and deep to aid in your visualization. This exercise will soothe and calm you. It will open you up for the day and support you in being more attentive, receptive, and more willing to take action.

Activating Affirmations

Affirmations are another important practice. We have our own that we say daily, and we have affirmation cards from our favorite teachers.

We can all use words of support from others, but creating these words or phrases *ourselves* is perhaps even more important than getting them from someone else. Positive affirmations with pure intention and focused attention behind them are also key aspects to reconditioning negative thinking patterns and beliefs.

The more you are aware of yourself and the goodness you provide, the more bountiful your world becomes.

To use affirmations, say the ones you choose every morning when you awake, or when you're in the shower, or brushing your teeth. There is no right place, just as long as you say them in the morning, because it is a great way to start your day.

It's also important that you speak your affirmations aloud. You may feel self-conscious about this, and if you do, find more privacy. Just re- member, saying something positive about yourself isn't a bad thing! You are not creating delusions of grandeur or trying to feed your ego. Many people have difficulty accepting their basic decency, and it is only right (and it is the only way forward) that you recognize the enormous good that exists in you. Keep track of how many times you say your affirma- tions. Practice them all day if you wish. As you shift and transform, so may your affirmations.

In our experience, affirmations only work if you believe in them and live them. The reconditioning of your mind, emotions, and negative thought patterns are a crucial step in discovering your Gifts. Being pres- ent to your presence—to be deeply aware of where you are at any given moment—and being open, grateful, and flexible are all aspects that, when combined, create a strong foundation in the journey of discovery.

Look over the following examples of affirmations, and then choose something that works for you (feel free to create your own, too):

- I am a Gift, and everything about me was meant for con- structive and loving use!
- I am available to more good than I've ever imagined.
- I can do this.
- I am a cocreator of positive energy.
- I am a channel for good to unfold in the world, both for myself and others.
- The world was blessed the day that I was born; no one else can bring what I bring!
- The universe creates through me; my personal ideas are instruments of evolution.
- I claim betterment, love, peace, truth, authentic relation- ships, and personal power.

NIURKA: The foundation of the power of affirmations comes from the belief that we have that quality already. The quality of our life is directly proportional to the quality of our communication. We are continu- ally communicating: with our words, with the energy that underlies our words, with our physiology, with our eyes, with our heart. Affirmations are very powerful. They are not a tool, but more a way of thinking and being that elevates our frequency to better connect us to the universal energy.

There is nothing you do to someone that you are not doing to your- self. There is nothing that you give to someone that you are not giving to yourself. So, if you really want something in your life, like love, then give that.

STEP 4: INFINITE FEEDBACK

Green Mandala
Sharing and Reciprocity = Green Lotus Sparkles

•　　•　　•

A Gift is only a Gift if you create it—and then share it.

— MARK VICTOR HANSEN

If we don't give the Gift, we're killing ourselves.

— MICHAEL BERNARD BECKWITH

What the infinity feedback loop means to me is that when I am in my zone, when I am living my Gifts, I am in that loop, and I'm just flowing with the rest of infinity. There isn't anything else.

—JANET BR AY ATTWOOD

Step 4, infinite feedback, is the principle that the universe is continually showing you how you're doing. The world is a mirror reflecting who you're being. There is a constant loop of energy connecting you and the world around you. We call this loop *the infinity feedback loop of creation.* Imagine it like an infinity symbol. Or the number 8. It is profoundly im- portant that you become aware of what and why you are giving, as it will have a direct effect on what the universe is giving back to you. Getting your mind into this state is the result of your practice of being present to your own presence.

The universe will respond to your intent by allowing you to reap what you sow to teach you a lesson. It's like tending to your garden. The more love and care you give it, the better chance you have of a successful har- vest. So too do we have to tend to our Gifts. Hence the phrases: You get what you give. As above, so below. The more you give, the more you get.

When we share our inner light with those around us, it inspires oth- ers to do the same, and it feeds back to us the quality of who we are being.

Transformation and Energy

Everything is energy. You are in a constant energetic exchange with ev- erything else. There is a unified field of awareness and existence that is already and always in cocreation with itself and everything else. At the very core of your being, you *are* this unified field.

What is important to note again about this step is that the energy you put in, you get back. If you put negative energy into the loop, you can expect even more negative energy back. Better, obviously, to put in positive energy. In other words, all that negativity that you think is com- ing at you from "out there" is actually coming from inside you! The negativity you are feeling *is* the negativity you are giving off.

Michael Bernard Beckwith teaches us that our thoughts are mental energy, and Terry Tillman acknowledges that energy follows thought, so as seekers of our Gifts armed with knowledge, we need to be cognizant of these lessons. Each small choice we make plants a seed that has the potential to blossom and bear fruit. Therefore, it becomes imperative that we become and remain conscious of what seeds we're planting. If you want to harvest fruits that will feed your family, uplift humanity, and create a beneficial presence, then the seeds of love, joy, acceptance, peace, gratitude, harmony, understanding, and compassion must be planted and cared for, instead of the seeds of cynicism, resignation, despair, anger, anguish, rage, fear, doubt, and worry.

TRANSFORMATIONAL WISDOM

DEMIAN LICHTENSTEIN: By living my desire to become a spiritual and compassionate human being, I gained access to love, and in return I received love, and I got to feel whole. Then I felt the need to share my new Gift in a much bigger way. I wanted everyone to have access to the healing I experienced. This breakthrough into compassion transformed my notion of what I wanted to say to the world, and I began to make *Discover the Gift,* the motion picture, and to write this book.

SONIA POWERS: You probably already know something about reci- procity, since all religions teach it: what you give out, you get back. So in giving your Gift, you probably wonder what's in it for you. The answer is that you are in it for *you.* That is called complete knowingness: not *believing,* but *knowing* that whatever you're giving to another person, or to the world, you will get back. Now you may not get it back today, and you may not get it back from the person you're giving it to, but I promise you, whatever you give will come back to you. But if you hold back, then the universe will hold back from you, and you won't get to participate fully in this magnificent life. The more you give your Gift, the more you are yourself, the more you participate and make a difference in the world, the more the world will make a difference for you. The more people around you will want to be around you and share their Gifts. The more you will benefit. I promise.

HIS HOLINESS THE DALAI LAMA: There are official titles such as the "Temple Leader of Tibet" or "the Government" or even "Spiritual Leader." That kind of title I feel is sometimes a hindrance for having closer relations with different people. I really want to be just a simple Buddhist monk. That's my selfish motivation. Then I'd get genuine free- dom! I don't want to have this different title. Then there is my service, and its availability. In a Tibetan or any human community, if I can do something, I'm always available, so long as I am still breathing. I'm ready, wherever I can, to serve, including serving the Chinese as human brothers and sisters.

JACK CANFIELD: When you share your Gift, you actually increase your productivity, because when you hold yourself back, it creates an energy blockage in the environment. We see this in business, where people are afraid to give. Or they're in it for the money. Or they don't work for the love of the job. I want a gardener who loves to garden. I want a cook who loves to cook. I want someone who loves cars to work on my car, not somebody who's just doing it to make money. And when we're doing what we love, the hours flow by and we get more productive.

When you regard sharing your Gift as a philosophy of life and won- der, "Why does it work? Why is it important?" it's this: each of us is like a cell in a larger human body, and when each cell does its job, the body works. If my kidney cells stop working, my brain's in big trouble. If my liver cells stop working, if my heart cells stop working, if my digestive system doesn't work, what happens? Every cell in my body is critically important. As such, each human being is critically important to the ful- fillment of humanity, our destiny, our joy.

It's a commitment to excellence that forces us to grow, and to not back away when it's tough. That's the deeper satisfaction. We're fulfilled by giving our Gifts. When you serve, you blossom. I don't think it gets any better than that.

You get out what you put in. Sometimes I get letters from people in prison, and they write, "Your book changed my life." (A book that I rewrote seven times.) "I used to blame everyone for being in prison, but now, as a result of reading your book, I realized I'm responsible for being in prison. As a result of that, I've changed my attitude. I'm treating the guards better. I'm asking them how their weekends went. They're treat- ing me better. Everyone in the cellblock wants me to be their counselor because they ask, 'How can you be in prison and be so happy?'"

These letters make me feel great. I gave my Gift and got a Gift in return.

MICHAEL BERNARD BECKWITH: The first evolutionary stage is learning how to give. People give in order to get something back. As we grow and we mature, we realize that we live to give. That's our purpose. When we begin to share our Gift, the universe corresponds to that vi- bration. The things of the world come to us a lot easier. Why? There's no resistance. We're not trying to "get" the things from the world; what we're doing instead is sharing. As we share our Gift, the resistance to whatever model that we're living in falls away, and we can say to our- selves, "You know, I want to experience more love in my life. I want to experience more abundance and prosperity. I want to have a greater health and creativity."

My priority is sharing. My priority is giving. My priority is releasing life energy. My priority is radiating. My priority isn't getting.

If I go to getting, then I resist the very thing that I want. So, as I hone my Gift, what am I doing? I'm building my consciousness of *I am* and *I have.*

The universe responds to that.

I am. I have. Things show up. It's not magical. It is part of the unified field, where everything is working together for my good.

DEMIAN LICHTENSTEIN: Discovering my Gift is one thing. Living it . . . that is something else. It requires as much focus and dedication as anything I've ever done. It is a challenge to every fiber of my being to be in service to what I am becoming. The more I studied and meditated on sharing my Gifts, the more the universal spiritual steps continued to unfold within my being. And once again

I awakened to this unified field of awareness where everything was connected in perfect vibrational harmony with everything else. As I became open and receptive to this in- finite loop of energy, I realized that the more I shared my Gifts, the more it inspired others to share their Gifts. I was feeding them, and they were feeding me. There was a universal, spiritual principle at work: the infinity feedback loop of creation.

JOHNNY MADONIA: As a personal development specialist, I would say my Gift is my ability to help people become more integrated in their mind, body, and spirit. I coach and train high-level executives to use their brains and their bodies for maximum capacity. I have coached top boxers as well as multimillionaires who hold themselves to a very high standard and maintain themselves at world champion status. I see men from the age of nineteen all the way up to forty-eight and forty-nine years old. I've also worked with race car drivers, body builders, and seventy-five-year-old women who have arthritis. I help them eliminate their pain, since it's a mental thing.

Sure, we feel pain physically; there are demonstrably physical reasons why. But if I can get into the mental part and show people how to rise above their pain, rise above the obstacles, I can show them how they no longer have to feel the pain. My Gift is teaching them how their brain can heal their body.

I was coaching one man all through law school, and the way he kept his mind alert was through boxing. He studied and took tests at night for the bar exam and trained physically all day. It all worked together, and I think that my role in his life was not just to tell him how many weights to lift but to show him that being in tune with himself, mentally and physically, he could achieve anything. The fact that he went from a high level of boxing workout to a high level of studying, in the same day, just proves my point of mind over matter.

Removing the blockage in people's brains allows the light to "snap" in their head. Instantly they say, "Wow!" and they suddenly see it. It's that moment, even though they may have thought about it every day for twenty years. It finally clicks in their head and they say, "Oh yeah, now I understand!" That's the most beautiful thing in the world. I love being able to help them turn on that light switch. The mind controls the body, and the goal is achieved very quickly. You see it very clearly, when an hour ago you might have thought you never could have done it; now you can.

NIURKA: When we're giving, we're coming from a premise of abun- dance, and we're acknowledging that abundance, and that acknowledg- ment creates the space for even more abundance to flow into our lives. There's nothing that you give that you won't experience. It's like if you smile at someone, you get the Gift of feeling the smile. Or if you give the Gift of laughter, you're the one who's laughing. Or if you give the Gift of love, you're feeling the love because it's flowing through you and it comes back.

SHAJEN JOY AZIZ: I always wanted to create possibility in the lives of children, and I did it in many ways as an educator, school counselor, and mental health professional. To be perfectly honest, though, I always wanted to do it on a much larger scale. And now here I am doing it in ways I never would've known possible before. You are in the midst of a global movement about discovering your Gift, your true essence, and who you are. This is going to impact you on a personal level, your fami- lies, your communities, and ultimately the children.

I've learned that I love writing books and making documentaries, be- cause the process is about educating. Now I get to educate about the discovery of ourselves and our Gifts through mass media and on levels that really hit home, where people from all over the world can connect with one another. When I finally chose to be who I really am and to serve in the ways that energized me as well, the world opened up, and the universe said, "Yes, we're ready for you." And my life, as I know it today, unfolded. It was that simple *and* that hard.

CHERIF AZIZ: When I started valuing my own self, my heart, my time, my dream, it was as if I came out of a cave and finally, finally started liv- ing in light. Shajen and I just started having another level of relationship. It was amazing.

DEMIAN LICHTENSTEIN: When you engage in the discovery of your Gift, you activate the unlimited potential within your own being. As you continue to discover and hone in on that never-to-be-repeated-in-all- of-creation miracle that you are, you then begin to experience a life of power, fulfillment, joy, freedom, bliss, and love. As you nurture and edu- cate your Gifts as you would your own child—understanding that your Gifts must go through stages of growth and development—this experi- ence of deep meaning and being a beneficial presence on the planet will become real for you, and you will begin to see the Gift in everything and everyone.

On the other hand, if you choose to ignore your Gifts and choose not to acknowledge them in yourself, in others, or the circumstances of your life, then in the infinity feedback loop of creation you will experi- ence the opposite: resignation, cynicism, pain, despair, rage, and confu- sion. This is the energy that you will feed into the loop. It will be your ongoing experience of life.

CHRISTINE STEVENS: When you start to use your Gift to serve, magic happens in your life. It's like a soloist becoming a part of a band. It's like being part of a choir of angels. One of the most spiritual mo- ments for me is feeling the connection between people I thought were my enemies and myself, not making my music or their music, but coming together and forming something new, a new song.

JANET BR AY ATTWOOD: Have you ever tried hard to be something you're not? I can't tell you how many doors I've closed trying to tweak myself so I would be what I thought others were looking for. Some- one really important comes into your life, and all of a sudden you're shape-shifting. In a world of abundance, we don't have to shape-shift anything. The people looking for *you* are going to find you. What is so cool about being you is that you're showing up authentically.

CHRISTINE STEVENS: When you don't use your Gift, it's like talking with your hands over your mouth. It's the greatest game of hide-and-seek!

Look for it, find it, and be it. You don't have to play it, just be it. A trans- formation happened for me when I realized that music is not something I *played;* it's something I *am.* Saint Francis said it this way: "Make me an instrument of peace." I think we're moving from make *me* an instrument of peace to make *us* the instrument of peace. So the more people who are waking up to their Gifts and contributing, the more we are all trans- forming together. It's about us! It's about we.

For me, I went from being a go-getter to a go-giver, and I went from being a performer to being a reformer. And those transformations hap- pened by just following my Gift, by jamming, by making my own music, not the music somebody else told me to play, but just jamming what was in my heart. You know how jamming is: you just let go and flow, and you find other jamming partners in life, and all of a sudden there's a sym- phony that's happening.

SIR KEN ROBINSON: There's an old expression about being an "Indian giver," which is supposed to describe someone who gives you a Gift and then wants it back. It seems like the opposite of generosity. But the tradi- tion that underpins this understanding comes from the Native American and aboriginal communities. You give a Gift in the expectation that the person will receive it for a while and enjoy it and then hand it on to somebody else so they can enjoy it too. A Gift is part of the sacred pro- cess of sustaining the community and sharing the wealth.

This kind of sharing is really what lies behind the idea of discovering your Gift. You are not discovering it just for yourself. It is for you to offer to other people. In offering it to other people, you're build- ing a stronger sense of community between yourself and the people with whom we share the earth. It's part of contributing to and being part of the commonwealth of humanity. In that respect, discovering your own Gifts is an act of being selfless, as well as one of fulfilling yourself.

HIS HOLINESS SRI SRI R AVI SHANKAR: Anything we do in our lives, we do with the expectation of receiving some happiness, some pos- itive result for ourselves. We find some Gift deep within us, and then we want to express it, to share it with everyone. It makes all the difference in our life when we shift from this position of expecting something to sharing what we can with the world.

Looking within, I discover I have all that I need for myself, and now I am going to share it with others. The joy of wanting to have things is natural. We are born with it. We all see that as children we want to have something more. But that joy has to mature and become the joy of shar- ing. It's like the grandmother and the grandfather and the love they share with their grandchildren. The joy of sharing is much more life-fulfilling. It is good to move from wanting to sharing.

ANDREW SOLIZ: Some people are storytellers, some people are musi- cians, and some people are caregivers. Whatever your Gift is, that is the thing you are meant to develop within yourself and to share with the world. Like any Gift, it doesn't mean as much if you just hold on to it and keep it to yourself. The true Gifts are the ones that we receive and give back to the world in whatever way is necessary. For me, people say that the Gift I have is to run ceremonies to help people learn about themselves. It's something I didn't choose to do; it was chosen for me, I believe by the spirits. However, I did choose to live a life that developed the necessary skills so I can give back in an appropriate way, in a respect- ful way. In a way that does good things for myself, my loved ones, or anybody who chooses to come to that ceremony.

DAVID "AVOCADO" WOLFE: To me, the ultimate Gift that one per- son can give to another is inspiration. Inspiration is an energy, a wave form. When we're in that perfect frequency of what we're supposed to be doing, we can get into a state of perpetual chills going up and down our back. A perpetual state of inspiration.

MICHAEL BERNARD BECKWITH: There's a statement, I think from the Gospel of Thomas, in which Jesus is saying something to the effect that "As you give your Gift, it will free you and liberate you. If you don't give your Gift, it will kill you." In other words, there is something seeking to emerge through all of us as we activate our potential.

PERSONAL PRACTICES

DAVID "AVOCADO" WOLFE: Practice saying "Today is the best day ever!"

FATHER GREG APPARCEL: Sometimes you learn more about yourself by what you teach other people, not what they teach you.

JACK CANFIELD: The affirmation that reminds me of who I am and what I'm about is this: "I am standing in the light of God, sharing my living love with everyone I meet." My purpose statement in life is "to inspire and empower people to live their highest vision, in the context of love and joy."

JANET BR AY ATTWOOD: Transcendental meditation is something that is taught in a very systematic way, by a teacher of meditation. The teacher gives you what's called a mantra, a meaningless sound that has the ability to take your awareness within. I wish I could just tell you how to do it, but you have to do it yourself. We're so used to all of our senses being out here, and what we need is to redirect within. The mantra fills you with a deeper calm, a deeper state of peace, a deeper sense of con- nection and silence. But don't take my word for it, go find yourself a transcendental meditation center—or some form of meditation that has a tradition to it, meaning it's lasted over time and has retained its value. And then practice it, just like brushing your teeth every day, twice a day.

You probably don't even look to see if your teeth are clean afterward; it's automatic. Meditation works that way, too.

GROWTH OPPO RTUNITIES

Awareness

Pause and revisit the breathing techniques described on pages 89 and 106.

Become present to your breath, to this moment, to your body, and to this journey you are on. Your source, your inner wisdom, is constantly speaking to you. Your source relays messages that can guide your internal compass and point you in the direction of your dreams. The more you are able to tune in to your source, your inner wisdom, your soul, and the more you are able to act on this inner knowledge, the more joyful your life will be.

As you take a deep breath, breathe in gratitude and allow it to permeate every cell of your being. Use your imagination to visualize fresh air filling your body. As you release your breath, breathe out any negative emotions or thoughts you have been holding on to. With your next breath, breathe in light and love. Again visualize the light, and as you exhale, breathe out anger, confusion, and darkness. Anytime you have a moment to become present and breathe in goodness and gratitude and breathe out negativity and confusion, please do. This practice will help to keep a clear path for your inner knowledge to manifest itself.

Know that you are on the path to self-discovery. You can accomplish anything you desire through being present to your presence—aware of yourself, of your actions and choices, and having clear intentions about the things you know to be most important to you.

What we have learned is that our journey in this lifetime is about self-realization and self-appreciation, acceptance, and understanding. The more we are able to love and accept ourselves, the more we are able to love and accept others. We believe that love is the ultimate essence we are all striving for, whether we are aware of it or not. Our lives are made up of many peaks and valleys, and it is at the heart of both the highs and the lows that our true nature shines forth.

Your journey is about fully understanding your uniqueness, and con- necting with new ways of thinking and being. To support this journey I want to share how important it is to recondition and work on your mind and your emotions, to connect them in powerful and positive ways. Use your journal to record your ideas and feelings and any intuitive insights that come to you. Revisiting your journal and your inner knowing con- nects you to your source. Pay attention to any repeating themes that emerge from your writing. Many times, the key to your Gift is wait- ing in those lines. Following are a few suggestions to help you in your journaling.

Journaling Ideas

Your Life as a Movie

Think of your life as a movie, then write the script and direct it on the page. The story could be about your old life or about the new life you want to embark on. Who are the characters in your story? Where does it take place? Where do you want it to take place? What are the protago- nist's goals, meaning, what are your goals? What are some possible pit- falls? Who are the adversaries? Where does tension come in? What kind of score does your movie have? Is it in black and white or high-definition color? As you write your story, pay attention to what you're focusing on and also to what you are leaving out. Then roll the credits. What is your response to your work? How can you bring those scenes to life? How can you share them with others?

Finding Your Assets

An asset is a valuable quality or resource. It is here that we want you to look inside and ask yourself what you think are your valuable qualities. We request that you be truthful with yourself, and we want you to know that it is through your authenticity that your Gifts become revealed. List at least eight assets, including only the ones that feel authentic to you.

Ask yourself the following questions:

- What does my source say?
- What am I meant to do?
- What is working for me in my life right now?
- If I could do anything I want as a career, and money was not an object, what would I choose to do?

Now go back and write your answers. Write your heart out! Make it a prayer, a meditation, a game, a call to action. Write and don't worry about the words or punctuation or grammar. Just pour yourself out on the page. When you are done, ask yourself how you can give your assets to others. Maybe this can be achieved by sharing an inspirational story or using your talents as a designer to help someone beautify a home, and in turn, inspire that person to discover their Gifts. We can certainly hold on to whatever it is we think is precious about ourselves, but that's not how we grow. If you want to see your world blossom in front of you, find a way to give your assets away. It's an investment in your future.

Take Action

Here are a few suggestions on how you can begin to share your Gifts:

1. Share your gratitude with those you love and those who have taught you important life lessons.
2. Go and find a conference or workshop where you can openly share who you are and be open to learning from others.
3. Volunteer at a hospital, homeless shelter, animal shel- ter, or school.
4. Become a foster parent.
5. Write a letter to a friend or relative you haven't spoken to in a long time.
6. Be bold and express yourself to others through dance, music, and art.

7. Create a nonprofit organization.

8. Donate your time to a favorite charity.

9. Give out at least thirty-nine hugs a day. It's good for the heart.

10. Part of sharing your Gifts is about being authentic. As you find places where you can share what lights you up and inspires you, start building the muscle of being "a passion magnet," as Janet Bray Attwood teaches us. Practice giving your Gift to others on a daily basis. If your Gift is to be a writer, then write words of inspira- tion to a friend. If your Gift is to serve, then be on the lookout for ways to help friends and strangers. Maybe it's simply holding the door for someone or picking up a pair of gloves that someone has dropped on the subway. Each of these giving actions takes seconds of your time but could change a person's life forever.

STEP 5: VIBRATION

Blue Mandala
Vibration/Energy = Blue Lotus Sparkles

• • •

There's a principle in music called "sympathetic vibration." When I play my drum, another drum nearby will also vibrate at that same pitch and will be played without anyone touching it. When we hear a pulse, we can't help but join it. Life wants to harmonize. Every beat, every note we make, is felt somewhere.

— CHRISTINE STEVENS

My brother and I grew up always hearing about whether we were giving off good vibes or bad vibes. Thus we've always been really clear about how our vibrations interact with the rest of the world and how they affect us and other people. So, again, do you want to project good vibes or bad vibes? That is what vibration is all about, the kind of being you are in the world, the energy that you put out into the world. We want you to be really clear about what that means and how you contribute "your vibes" to the planet.

— SHAJEN JOY AZIZ

The entire universe is one vibrational machine. Nothing is at rest, no matter how it looks. Everything in the universe moves, vibrates, swirls, and travels in circular and spiral patterns—even our DNA.

This same principle applies to our thoughts, feelings, desires, and dreams. Everything, every thought, as well as all energy, has a unique vi- brational frequency, from planets to nails on a blackboard to your voice in the shower. Animals hear sounds we can't, their eardrums vibrating to different frequencies, and bats use echolocation. Music is all about vibra- tion. How many of us are in tune with the song the universe is singing? Quantum physicists know this vibrational paradigm as "string the- ory," a way of describing the nature of the universe as made up of in- finitesimally tiny multidimensional vibrating "strings." The frequency at which they vibrate gives them form.

Tuning In to Your Own Vibrations

It is imperative that you get in tune with your own vibration and under- stand that the energy you send into the universe has a direct effect on your entire existence. As a matter of fact, your own vibration is actually cocreating the world that you perceive in front of you. Your emotions create a frequency. Your thoughts create a frequency. Combined they give off a unique vibration, resonating together like strings of a guitar. Now, sometimes those notes sound harsh, sometimes they sound beautiful. So much of it has to do with where you are at any given moment in your life.

We live in our medium of energy even though we may not perceive it.

Like water for fish, energy holds us, propels us, and gives us life.

Although this step holds that everything is in perpetual dynamic movement, we do have the power within us to use, effect, and channel that energy in order to alter our lives. Higher vibrations consume and transform lower ones; because of this we can change the conditioning of our mind and emotions and thus the energies in our lives. And this change can be perpetual, because according to the law of the conserva- tion of energy, energy never dies; it simply changes state and form. Move matter at the speed of light squared, and it becomes energy.

It is our greatest desire that you are able to know about and tap into the array of cosmic forces that are at your fingertips awaiting your arrival.

You now have the opportunity to discover your Gift in terms of the infinite energy available to you. We want you to know that you have the power to shift your thinking and actions by being open and aware. This openness will bring you to a greater awareness of yourself, your mind, your emotions, and how you have been conditioned by yourself, your family, your community, your education, and, most important, by what you make your life circumstances mean.

You now have the choice to tune in to the frequencies of joy, happi- ness, and fulfillment. Which are you going to choose first?

TRANSFORMATIONAL WISDOM

JACK CANFIELD: We call ourselves "human beings" and not "human doings," because what we're really bringing into any situation is the vibra- tional quality of our being. When we're being loving, inclusive, expres- sive, joyful—all these create vibrations. The same with negative emotions and actions. Everything is translatable into energy. It's the quality of the energy, the enthusiasm or lack of it, the love or lack of it, the anger or lack of it, that really has the most impact.

DEMIAN LICHTENSTEIN: As I began moving along a deeper path, sharing from my heart, the world began showing up completely dif- ferently for me. Whatever I gave out came back. I noticed the many dimensions of energy, and other laws of the universe, that affect our lives every second. We coexist in a dynamic energy field, a feedback loop of creation, and we are all one with it. Our vibrational presence is always making a difference.

B ARBARA DE ANGELIS: When you show up, who shows up? It doesn't matter what you're thinking. It doesn't matter what you want to say. First, people will *feel* your vibration and everything you've brought in- to that moment. In keeping with the cyclical, feedback nature of the universe, whatever you're vibrating you're going to get back. Anger, re- sentment, shame: all are vibrations. Peace, happiness, love: the same. Emotions are really just vibrations, and if they're not vibrating at the highest and most expansive level, you will actually push away what's try- ing to come to you.

DEMIAN LICHTENSTEIN: You need to look in the mirror. You need to look inside your own being to discover where your vibe is off. Where is your anger, despair, cynicism, resignation? You've got to come to terms with those vibrations before you can vibrate positively into the world.

B ARBARA DE ANGELIS: At every moment, we are either expanding or contracting. For instance, if you're feeling angry, blaming somebody, feeling sorry for yourself, you'll feel yourself contract. If you're thinking about offering, helping, compassion, you feel expansive. When you meet somebody, you can instantly feel if they have good or bad "vibes." It's not a mistake that we have made that "hip" terminology part of our vernacular. Because what are you actually feeling if not a vibrational im- print, the sum total of every thought, every feeling, every action that that person has had?

NIURKA: We've all met someone who tended to be a bit negative even if something great has happened in their life. They say, "Well, this is great, but not for long."

And you say, "Not for long? What are you talking about? Something great just happened!"

Their belief system is grounded in negativity, and despite their infinite Gifts they will vibrate that negativity in the universe until it comes back to them in what we call a self-fulfilling prophecy. It's like somebody walking out of their house on a beautiful California day and say- ing, "Well, here's another lousy day in paradise." Unless they're making a joke, they are unaware of what they are creating through their language. They are literally calling that into existence through the vibration and their choice of words. So it is essential to realize in discovering our Gifts and living them that we create as we speak.

RICK ROSS: When you show energy, when you vibrate in a positive way, people really like to be around you. Do you know what I'm saying?

Nobody wants to be around stagnation or negativity. They want to see something moving, something going on. That's attractive. When I carry this energy, this light, this sparkle with me, then like gravity it tends to pull in all the things that I want with it. Friends, relationships, money. It all comes through that energy. This is why it's not good to think negatively, because when you do, the exact thing that you're thinking about is drawn to you. When they teach race car drivers how to drive, they teach them not to look at the wall that they are going toward, because whatever you're looking at is what you're going to be drawn to.

SCOTT PETERSEN: Most people don't react from the center. In other words, they don't treat things as important because they like them; they treat things as important because they have a title or deep pockets. And they end up creating a whole bunch of malignancies because instead of reacting from the heart, they're reacting from some overlaid mental program.

B ARBARA DE ANGELIS: We vibrate things into our life. We vibrate things out. We vibrate people in. We vibrate people out. We vibrate op- portunities in. We vibrate opportunities out. But is there a difference be- tween living as a positive vibrational being and being a positive thinker? I think so. It means cleaning out our vibration of everything that is not serving us. It means raising our vibration with love, with all the things that we know expand us and make us feel that we're vibrating at a higher frequency.

PENNEY PEIRCE: Music is a vibration, and in life, once you choose— let's call it your tone—your life starts to be created out of and around that tone. If you choose a low tone, you get a low-level life with a lot of snags and problems. If you rise up and move into the higher frequencies, you get a new understanding of reality in which everything's much more unified.

DAVID "AVOCADO" WOLFE: I learned an incredibly powerful question from Marshall Rosenberg, the man behind *Nonviolent Communication*. He said, "What is the outcome of your communication?" That's been turn- ing over in my head ever since the moment I heard it. If I get emotionally aggressive because my mom starts yelling at me about something, I re- mind myself that the outcome of this communication—the reason why I'm here with my mom—is to share an experience of love, support, and appreciation with her. If she starts yelling at me and I yell back to her, that is not taking me any closer to this goal. This concept has helped me immensely in business, in emotional relationships, and in relationships with my family.

DEMIAN LICHTENSTEIN: We're simply a vibration held together in this bodily form, and we're able to express ourselves, to experience con- sciousness, to experience this tactile world, to eat, to love, to laugh, to raise families, to create grand edifices, to have art and music. To get this, truly get this, is extraordinary!

NIURKA: I always say your communication is the response you get! If you want someone to know how much you love them, but the vibration and energy of your communication elicit anger and resentment from an- other, then that is the communication you delivered, regardless of what you think it was.

PERSONAL PRACTICES

HIS HOLINESS SRI SRI R AVI SHANKAR: Go within, relax, just be with nature. That is what connects us with the universal spirit. I tell you it's not difficult. Many people think it is very difficult to be mindful, but all it needs is just a little recognition, a little recognition of body, breath, mind, and intellect—of what the intellect is saying, of whether we are agreeing or disagreeing within ourselves, of how we are responding. A simple awareness.

When you lose enthusiasm, when you are tired, when you are physi- cally tired, mentally tired, emotionally worn out, that is when you feel it's hopeless. That's when you have no energy to even think about an adventure. But even when we face an obstacle, what seems to be an ob- stacle, in those moments I would say we have to rest, relax, go deep within. That is when meditation comes into play. You know, when we meditate, we relax, and suddenly we find a spring of energy within us. A great source of enthusiasm coming out of us.

Go within, and relax, just be with nature. That is what connecting with the universal spirit is all about.

There are three things we need to understand. One is compassion, compassion for all life. Second is commitment in life, commitment to good for all. And third is connectivity. We are connected to the universe. We are connected to everybody.

Whether you like someone or not, you are still connected. Space itself connects us, as do air and water and the sun. The earth itself connects us.

Feel compassion in that connectivity.

Feel commitment for good in life, for all that is evolutionary, pro- gressive in life, for all that brings so much happiness in life.

The whole world is vibration. Everything is vibration.

When we become more compassionate, committed, and connected, then the happy, peaceful, and calm vibration emits from us. It draws similar situations to us. The universe brings back to us the Gifts we give.

When we connect with the universal presence, our life becomes an effortless expression of joy.

Rather than expecting joy from the universe, we start emitting those vibrations of happiness from within ourselves.

ANDREW SOLIZ: Stop trying to make your life choices from the sur- face. Go into your heart, not your mind. Your mind will always trick you. Your heart will always be true. Your heart will speak through your mind with fullness and positivity. Your mind speaks with fear. Your heart will tell you instantly what that answer is, and in another instant your mind will come in and say, "Yeah, but, maybe, what if. . ." Our tendency is to be afraid of the heart, but the fear lives in the mind. When you find the peace in yourself and walk your truth and always stay in your heart, your life will be easier, much easier.

GROWTH OPPORTUNITIES

Expansion and Contraction

Have your journal handy for this exercise.

1. First, begin from a place of contraction. Think about a recent event in which you felt angry, blaming, or sorry for yourself.
2. Notice your body and how it feels. Is it open and expansive, or is it closed and contracted? Write down at least two sensations you felt, and jot down your thoughts, feelings, and "aha" moments.
3. Now begin from a place of expansion. Think about love, happiness, joy, your favorite people and places.
4. Notice your body and how it feels. Is it contracted and closed or open and expansive? Write down at least two sensations you felt, and jot down any and all emotions and ideas that come to mind. Allow all to be valid.
5. Breathe. Take a deep breath and begin to relax. Notice your entire body, all your sensations. Think about being present to

your presence, feel yourself and your inner core, listen to what your inner source reveals about your Gifts and your next steps.

6. Write down any and all thoughts, feelings, sensations, "aha" moments, upset—anything that comes to you.

Expanding Your Inner Guidance

Your body is a vehicle of communication for you, and it is essential as you take this journey that you pay attention to it and the vibrations that resonate within you. Listen to those messages. We encourage you to be open and honest with yourself, and your true essence and the discovery of your Gifts will shine through.

When you are ready, whether sitting or standing, align your back, hold your core in, close your eyes, and take a nice, relaxed breath. Make sure you exhale completely. Now do that again, although this time inhale a bit more, and then hold your breath for a second and feel that space. Now exhale and notice your presence, and with your next breath think back to a time that you were furious. Think about your body and its reaction to your upset. Your body contracted, everything became tight, agitated, and tense. Pay attention to those vibrations. Our goal is for you to feel expanded, loved, and open and excited to discover your Gift.

Now think of a time you felt the presence of calm serenity, and all was working smoothly in your life. Feel that sensation of expansion; notice your body and your mind. Notice the vibrations inside you. Breathe in all this good feeling, and breathe out any negative feelings or emotions.

With your next breath and every breath thereafter, we encourage you to continue to expand your awareness and be open to the greater good that flows through you.

As you expand your awareness, notice any and all thoughts, feelings, vibrations, and the like, and allow them to move through you. Do not hold on to any, just continue to breathe. When you are ready, notice your presence, and just be.

In your discovery journal write any and all thoughts, feelings, emo- tions, and experiences.

The Om Exercise

This exercise builds on the previous two exercises. For those of you not familiar with the om, it is a sacred sound that is prevalent in many

Eastern religions. It sounds exactly as it is written—*om*—although the "m" sound is usually elongated and held for a certain period of time. Some of you may have used the om for meditation, and we're sure that others of you have heard it used in movies or cartoons (it seems to be the stereotypical sound to make whenever someone is meditating on the big or small screen). It is a very important sound for many, however, and it is honored as the sacred sound of the universe.

The om exercise is a very powerful tool and one we can use to help us feel the vibrations in our bodies.

First, find a place where you can be alone and where you won't dis- turb anyone and no one will disturb you (we do not recommend doing this exercise while commuting on a bus).

Sit in a comfortable position. Take a few deep breaths and try to cen- ter yourself and calm your mind.

When you are ready, take a deep breath, breathing into your dia- phragm (your belly should protrude when you do so). Hold for a second or two, then as you exhale, chant or speak the sound *om,* and allow the sound to rise out of you, passing through your body from your core, up your chest, and out your mouth.

Pay particular attention to how your rib cage, your legs, your back, and your head vibrate to the sacred sound. Repeat this process, and again focus on how your body is vibrating to the sound emanating from your inner universe.

Continue to breathe and exhale *om,* and imagine that your body is vibrating along with the sacred sound of the universe. Imagine yourself becoming one with your source the way a musician playing her instru- ment to the direction of a conductor becomes one with the symphony.

As you *om,* you are becoming one with the universe, and together you are making beautiful music.

STEP 6: ADVERSITY AND TRANSFORMATION

Indigo Mandala
Adaptability and Transformation
= Indigo Lotus Sparkles

•　　•　　•

Adversity is the diamond dust Heaven polishes its jewels with.

— THOMAS CAR LYLE

The truth is, there is good in absolutely everything that happens. We signed up for this experience so that we could learn lessons. The things that we learn are to better us, to make us grow, to improve us, and to empower us, even if an experience seems to be negative at the time, even if it seems to be very sad or something that you might be fearful of. The truth is, if you look for the good—if you look for that good—it's there.

— SONIA POWERS

Tragedy. Failure. Loss. Rejection. Pain. Each of these events shocks and saddens us and weighs us down. But

Step 6, adversity and transforma- tion, is about understanding that there are Gifts in *all* circumstances.

Of course, adversity is not a word usually associated with a Gift. How is it possible that an unexpected outcome, a plan gone awry, or a personal betrayal is often a doorway to our greatest Gifts?

There are many events that we perceive as tragic and painful, that show up to stop us from what we think we want. If we focus on our disappointment, or how much we hurt, all we will feel is the pain, and that pain will keep us from being present to the idea that every one of these situations contains within it a turning point, a fresh start, a new beginning. A rebirth. In other words, you can think of adversity as marking the end of one stage and the beginning of an opportunity to advance to the next level. As it is said, "When God closes a window, He also opens a door." In this way, adverse outcomes, resistance to our best-laid plans, friends and peers who don't share our vision—all are pathways to the discovery of our own Gift and our own reason for being.

This step states that during our lifetime, each of us will encounter a certain level of adversity—a series of problems and challenges, if you will. You could call these occurrences tests of initiation, for the pur- pose of strengthening the light within. We must consider each of these tests to be a challenge and remain connected to our hearts when moving ahead. The greatest challenge will be your willingness in the face of ad- versity to open your heart again and again and again.

When you pay very close attention to adversity, you will recognize that it is extremely powerful. Your capacity to manifest is challenged be- cause it requires you to make a shift inside.

You can either choose to transform or allow the adversity to con- trol you.

Transforming Through Adversity

Everything in your life is there as a vehicle for your transfor- mation. Use it!

—*RAM DASS*

As we evolve, unfold, and transform, so do our Gifts and our ability to tune in to them and share them. Transformation may sound complicated, but this chapter demonstrates that it is a fairly straightforward matter of how we choose to see ourselves and others, and from there determining how we choose to think and act.

Have you ever watched a singer who entranced you? Did you wonder why she had that effect on you? Putting personal taste aside, it's because *she loves to sing*—she can't help it. This is her Gift and by sharing it with you, she affects you.

In the same way you have to actively share your Gift, and you will af- fect yourself, others, and the universe.

Life at its best is a series of ups and downs. It goes without saying that each and every person will encounter problems throughout their lifetime. This truth—however unpleasant it seems—is actually a path- way to the discovery of unseen Gifts. Life's adversities, though usually unwelcome, are many of the stepping stones along your journey.

During Demian's senior year in college, a creative tragedy rocked him to his core. He had spent over a year making his senior thesis film, *A Statue in Time.* Many people in our community contributed money and resources to this epic adventure, which was set in both medieval times and modern-day New York City. After he had completed pro- duction on the film that was sure to propel him into the career he had always dreamed of, a moment of neglect sent Demian's dream up in smoke. His life's work vanished, and Demian quite literally disappeared.

It took Richard, our father, two days to find him, and when he did, Demian was in total despair and on the verge of suicide. Richard took Demian into his art studio and had him paint a graph that represented his emotions. "Here, Son," Dad said, "put the brush on the canvas. Start- ing at the center here, if the top of the canvas is the highest you could feel and the bottom is the lowest, I want you to think back to when your movie was going to be made. How did you feel?"

Demian painted a line to the top.

Dad continued: "And when you discovered that the university might pull the plug because the project had gotten too big . . . how did you feel?"

Demian painted a line to the bottom. As Dad continued to ask ques- tions, the graph grew until Demian's entire emotional experience was painted before him. Then Dad said, "Now put the brush back on the canvas and draw a horizontal line in one motion." Demian did as he was told.

Both Dad and Demian then stepped back from the canvas, and Dad asked, "Do you know what that is, Son?"

"No, Dad, I don't . . . what is it?"

Richard responded with something we never forgot. "This is the life of a human being. You will experience the greatest heights and the lowest of lows. Your job is to always return to the center line."

Of course it isn't easy or part of conventional wisdom to regard your tragedies as breakthroughs to who and what you are. And who wants to hear from someone on the sidelines, even if it's a friend or loved one, that what's upsetting you is potentially a great Gift?

We can tell you that the depth of the pain we experienced when our mother died was one of the most defining moments of our lives. As Demian recalls, "I can tell you that identifying my mother's car and seeing the blood and the pieces of her inside that car was a very difficult moment for me. If someone had said to us then, 'Wow, your pain is a great Gift. Demian, you're going to be a filmmaker who creates great sto- ries, and, Shajen, you're going to be an educator and mother and maybe one day do something to change the world,' we would have told them to jump off a cliff. Or worse."

In retrospect, what happened changed our lives even more drastically than we ever thought. And, luckily, because our mother and father had already encouraged our Gifts from when we were very young, we in- nately, if not consciously, understood who and what we were. We had something we could hang on to—a stronger relation to our Gifts.

As Demian recalls: "My understanding of this law became part of me, even though I didn't know it was a law, in the aftermath of losing everything that I knew to be solid and real in life: my family structure; my home, which had burned down; and my mother, who had died. That rapid disintegration made it necessary for me to create a new life that had never existed prior to that moment. It wasn't a slow process, but an immediate need. Because I had within me the seeds of my Gift of being a filmmaker, I had something I could hang on to, something that gave me power in the face of tragedy. Maybe I wouldn't end up a filmmaker, but I knew deep down that I could trust my capacity as an artist. Because I had to move forward in a dire situation, I trusted myself to keep being able to do that."

As Shajen says: "Because of what I got from my parents as a child, this fueled in me a desire to be there for children, teenagers, and families who are suffering. I can connect and work with them and facilitate a shameless journey for them out of their darkness and into the light of freedom from that shame. Throughout my time as a school-based mental health counselor, colleagues regularly commented on my ability to get through to the roughest and most messed-up children and teenagers. Parents have written me numerous letters of thanks and appreciation for supporting their children and helping them to become liberated from their emotional pain. I am grateful for my experiences because they have helped me to be of service to others and myself."

Part of our purpose in *Discover the Gift* is to extend that strength to everyone, especially children. The more we can understand and nurture our own Gifts, the greater our ability to see and support them in others. You can influence people in their formative stages and give them ac- cess to the discovery of who and what they are, what their passion and their purpose in life is—and why they're even here on the planet. When tragedy happens (and it can happen), it is different for everybody. Your access to power and freedom during these difficult times is through your understanding of your Gift. This relationship to the divine and sacred part of you will always carry you through, even in your darkest hour.

There are Gifts in all circumstances, including adversity. Your re- sponse is a measure of your adaptability and willingness to be open to transformation. This step is a pathway to the discovery of unseen Gifts. Resistance is neither positive nor negative. It is just resistance. No matter how bad we perceive our situation to be, there is always possibility for change, because we can't have bad without good, light without darkness, life without death.

TRANSFORMATIONAL WISDOM

STEWART EMERY: This thing called transformation literally means "to transcend the limitations ordinarily imposed by form." It means to have experience independent of external circumstances. It's not a light switch, but you can transform if you're willing to do the work.

DEMIAN LICHTENSTEIN: Once you have your first true transforma- tional experience, what you suddenly become aware of is that there are more to have, and you get very excited about what is next. You wonder, "What have I still not seen about myself, the seeing of which would make a profound difference in my life?"

The answer was clear: learn, grow, transform, and that is exactly what I did. I sought numerous transformational experiences, seminars, and teachers. I continued to move through my blocks and my past-based paradigms to discover new levels of understanding about myself, others, and the world in which I live. In the process of engaging in transforma- tional work and my own inner being continually changing, I am honored to have had the opportunity to coach thousands of people, as they have all been teachers for me as well. I used to be a dark, angry, suppressed, and depressed person. But as transformations unfolded me, I started to change and become a more positive person who had more to contribute than previously realized. And the more I contributed to others, the more they were contributing to me.

Michael Bernard Beckwith says, "Be ready to let go of the old you. Be ready to drop the past paradigm." Often that means you're not going to hang out in the same place you once did. Sometimes it means not hang- ing out with certain people. Mostly he means be ready to shed patterns and beliefs that no longer support you and those around you.

Andrew Soliz, my American Indian brother and dear friend, says it best: "Trees don't hang on to their dead leaves. They let go of what no longer serves them."

I used to hang on to everything. Prior to my personal revelations and transformations, I was really tired all the time, and everything seemed really heavy and smelled bad. And when I began to transform, my eyes opened and I looked down—and what I saw in front of me was a large wheelbarrow filled with manure. That manure was my past, and I had been pushing it around in front of me everywhere I went. It didn't matter what situation I was in. A business deal: "Hi, my name is Demian, this is all my crap, and it's nice to meet you. Don't mind the smell." With a woman: "Hi, my name is Demian, this is all my crap from all my previ- ous relationships. I know it smells bad, but let's hang out in it because I can't wait to get to know you."

Then one day I understood that I could put down the wheelbarrow, take a step to the right or to the left, and walk right past it. I could leave my past where it belonged: behind me. And then a remarkable thing happened—I felt free and unburdened and my entire life opened up in front of me. I was no longer looking at manure, but an entire, beautiful field of possibility. So, when you meet the next lover, or business deal, or family member, make sure you're not pushing around a wheelbarrow of crap. You are open and free. And possibility rules the day.

SHAJEN JOY AZIZ: I experience transformation continuously. It's never been just one moment or specific event for me. Instead, the moments of transformation are like a piece of scaffolding—each new transformation builds upon the previous one and I feel myself gradually rising higher and higher. I do, however, remember an early moment in which I clearly understood the cycle and spirit of transformation.

When I was young, I was walking home from my friend's house in the country, about a mile away from our house. I was alone. I saw a dead tree fallen on the side of the road. I was surprised to see, there amongst the decaying wood and rotting earth, new life emerging. This piece of dead forest gave life (and a home) to many little animals. Suddenly I felt very connected to the circle of life. To how everything transforms. Death does not mean the end. Often it's the beginning. This was my big awakening that everything has a life cycle of its own, and as Bob Marley sang, "When one door is closed, many more is open." I really got it in that moment, and I continued on home, where I saw Mom in the garden. I knew I was late and was probably in trouble.

"You're late!" she said.

"I know, Mom," I said, "but I got it! I understand life!"

That confused her. Even though she was pissed at me, she wanted to know what I meant. I explained it to her, and a smile broke over her face. "Honey, you get it! You understand!"

"I do!" I said.

"That's why I teach you about the moon, the stars, and the earth, so you understand that everything is connected."

And then she said: "Now, you're in trouble, so get into the house!"

HIS HOLINESS SRI SRI RAVI SHANKAR: Life is like a river: water flows, it doesn't stop because there is a stone, it flows over it. And in due course, it even shapes the stone itself. It just needs a little perseverance, patience, and conviction that love wins. And will always win.

When we believe that we are separate and different from that univer- sal energy, that's when we get stressed. When we don't realize this Gift, we feel small, narrow, agitated, jealous, and unhappy. We reel in all these neg- ative emotions. Relax deep within yourself into that presence, appreciate, honor the life that is within us and in others. When we recognize the life force that is everywhere, then we begin to see everything in life as a Gift.

SONIA POWERS: I was in a car accident and pronounced dead. During this time I had the experience of *being* everything, of experiencing all of the important people in my life, whether they were alive or had passed on. I had time to talk with them, and it seemed like this went on for days. I also got to "go to the light." The light was overwhelming and beautiful and full of joy. I felt no judgment. People tell us that when we die, we will be judged and have to atone for everything. That's not my experience. I simply felt love. Beautiful, magnificent, all-encompassing love, and we were one. All of us were one.

HIS HOLINESS SRI SRI R AVI SHANKAR: It is very strange but true: Whenever calamity hits, people who may be completely divided by reli- gion, language, nationality, and much else come together. They start to feel as if they are one human family. We experienced this truth when the tsu- nami hit the coast of India and there were floods. Rich or poor, educated or uneducated, everybody had to come together, stay under one roof; peo- ple of all religions, faiths, and languages were trapped together and helped one another. It was so heartening to see there was so much compassion, so much love, and such a sense of belongingness in spite of this adversity.

When we appreciate life itself as a Gift, we don't have to wait for calamity to unite us and bring compassion in our hearts.

JOHN CAS TAGNINI: I was also challenged by the death of my mother, no doubt about that. But even more challenging was to find the Gift in it. Is there really a blessing in my mom passing? Can I honor a transition? Can I find where she is now? I knew she was in my heart, but one of the greatest challenges I ever had in my life was to go into my heart and find her there, as opposed to looking for her on the outside.

The Gift I got out of it was this: "Think past the illusion that there's a death and a life that are separate."

RITA GUEDES: Loss is one of the most difficult things to go through. I lost my best friend. What I learned from the experience is that life is good, it's beautiful, but you have to know how to live. I decided to enjoy each moment. We don't know when we're going to leave this place, so it's not too early to start to love, forgive, be connected, and try to be a good person.

TERRY COLE- WHITTAKER: The process of transformation happens every moment. It's dependent on how we perceive life. We can perceive life either from the spiritual zone or from the material, fear-based zone.

One time I was with a friend and said, "I had no idea it was such a dark, gloomy day. It's gonna rain."

"But, Terry," she replied, "it's a bright, sunny day." "No," I said, "it's not. It's dark."

"Terry, you're wearing dark glasses."

So I took my glasses off, and it was a bright, sunny day.

The lesson was that we see through a filter. When we see through a filter of fear, which is basically judging our lives by outward appearances, we live in a world of greed and miserliness.

I think it was Saint Paul who said we "see through a glass darkly." When we perceive life through dark glasses, through the filters of fear, lack, and limitation, we make our decisions based on fear.

Transformation denies that reality. Transformation comes in every moment we choose not to judge by appearances. We choose not to base our decisions on what appears to be, but rather to make our decisions based on who we are as spiritual beings.

When we wake up to who we really are and stay awake in every mo- ment, we are transformed.

MICHAEL BERNARD BECKWITH: We always know it's transforma- tion because it surprises us. It shocks us! If it doesn't surprise you, it's not transformation. When we are available to good, however you define it, transformation can occur. When you throw yourself open by asking empowering questions and by being willing to be more than you've ever thought you could be, you get surprised by the depth of what's inside of you! It's so potent. It's like free fall.

JOHNNY MADONIA: Every man, woman, and child has mental blocks, regardless of whether these blocks pertain to their profession, their sport, or just their general development. And early on in most all of us, something usually happens that creates a fear that's hard to let go of. Maybe some kid in school was mean to you, and it hurt so much that you climbed into a shell and never got out. You kept wearing that shell. You're wearing it still. I see this with people at the highest levels. My job is to let people know that they don't have to stay in that place. They can remove the shell and the fear.

When they are ready, transformation occurs. And then they say, "If only I had realized this earlier, I might have had a different life." They finally got it that it was all in their head and that now they are able to start achieving amazing feats.

You don't have to understand how it works. Just believe that it's going to work.

"Believe" is the key word. If you believe it, you can achieve it.

When I was ten years old, I was very small. I didn't participate in any sports, and I got beat up. Now I had been born with a broken shoulder and a heart murmur. I was blind in my right eye, so I had to wear glasses and a patch over my good eye to strengthen the bad eye. I can laugh about it now, but I used to get knocked down at the bus stop because I couldn't see kids on the other side of me. One day a kid pulled out chunks of my hair and scratched my eye. He was really mean.

This whole time, I wanted to box, but my father was against it be- cause of my heart. I told him I was going to do it with or without him, so he decided to get my cousins to teach me how to box. I kept the boxing to myself and also got into weight lifting as part of the training.

At school, kids noticed I had gotten bigger and stronger, and they asked lots of questions. By the time I turned fifteen, kids regularly asked me for physical advice. As I gave it, I started to realize that most peo- ple don't have physical problems—they have mental blocks, and these mental blocks are what prohibit them from doing what they really want to do.

I totally believe, after thirty-five years of coaching champions, that every single human being has a champion buried deep inside. And that champion wants to come out. I don't care if you want to be a champion fighter, a champion boxer, a champion musician, or a champion in busi- ness. Donald Trump and Steve Wynn would be considered champions of business. I know from my experience that they must have truly felt there was a true champion inside them. But they took it a step further and made it a belief. Once you have the belief system inside of you, I don't care what you want to do, you will achieve it. It's the belief and the believing that make for the achieving. It's where manifestation and transformation happen.

SONIA POWERS: You're sitting at a stoplight, and a truck hits you from behind! How did you cause that? It could be that you weren't paying attention; it could be that you could've done something differently. I would like to go a little further and look at it in a much more profound way. Unconsciously, your mind may have noticed that you needed to learn something. Perhaps it was about caring or about being more con- scious. Some people actually get sick because they need to know that they're loved. They get in accidents because they need to know that their family will come to them and prove to them that they are loved and they are worthy.

The idea is to take everything that happens to you and choose to say, "Okay, what's the lesson here? What's the Gift here? What was I trying to accomplish? How did I draw this to me? Why did I bring this into my experience? What was I trying to get from it?" People have that ability. It must be for a reason, because, to the best of my knowledge, animals don't. It's a wonderful Gift to take a situation we consider terrible and think, "I must, at some level, have wanted this to happen, needed this to happen to learn something that I didn't know, so I could go to the next level of awareness, of consciousness of the greatness that I am, and offer my Gift more fully.

MICHAEL BERNARD BECKWITH: Some of you are going through some very dark times. You don't see a way out. Your back is against the proverbial wall; you're at your wit's end. You don't know what to do. Some of you are in situations that are chronic; you've been in this tough place for so long that you think it's your lot in life.

This is how you get out of it: You don't go to wishful thinking—"I wish I weren't here, I wish I'd never done what I did to get here, I wish I were somewhere else, I wish I were someone else."

Instead, ask this question: "If this experience were to last a long time, what quality would have to emerge in my life for me to have peace of mind?" If you ask this question, the moment your attention goes to that quality rather than the "getting rid of" the so-called problem, in that moment you've come into harmony with the evolutionary impulse and you begin to free yourself to be able to share your Gifts. You're not trying to get "out" of the problem. You're trying to become more yourself.

That's the real deal. We want to become ourselves. Every time we become more ourselves, the problems at the previous level disappear. They're only there because we're not activating our potential.

JACK CANFIELD: We don't develop inner strength without obstacles. We don't gain lessons or wisdom without something to overcome. So I see every obstacle and delay as a Gift, because it forces me to grow.

BILL HARRIS: People think that if something happens that you don't want, then you have to feel bad. But you don't have to. It's only when you're running on autopilot that you automatically feel bad. You do have a choice when something goes wrong. Actually, all of us can think back to major positive turning points in our life—and these turning points always turn out to be what looked like a disaster at the time.

MARK VICTOR HANSEN: The Gift is a full-time opportunity to look at life and say, "Hey, whatever comes my way, I'm going to solve it." It's usually adversity that is the greatest Gift, as it allows us to transcend and find the seeds of our own greatness.

RITA GUEDES: Sometimes transformation and the Gift come through contact with someone I consider an enemy. A person who hurts me is sometimes doing me a favor, pointing me toward a way of self- improvement. Realizing that everything that seems bad is actually a learning experience has helped me to grow spiritually. It's helped me to be a better person for myself, for others, and for the universe.

ANDREW SOLIZ: Great suffering causes great awareness. It helps us to unite. It helps us to figure out how not to let certain things happen again. Through this understanding we can choose to see things as all bad, or choose to see situations as a beautiful way to learn. Many of us are hardheaded, and we have to learn the hard way. We've been a hardheaded society and a hardheaded culture for a very long time. We are about to receive some hardheaded lessons, and they are coming, because it has to happen.

PERSONAL PRACTICES

STE WA RT EME RY: I recently discovered that I have prostate cancer. After the initial shock, I noticed within ten minutes that I was looking for the blessing in it. That triggered a series of the most extraordinarily serendipitous events and experiences. I have new friendships, and there's now a closeness between myself and my wife of twenty years that just keeps getting better. We often thought it couldn't get any better—but it does. It has been just amazing.

CYNTHIA M. RUIZ: Everybody has people in their lives who don't agree with them. When I recognize these adversaries, the first thing that I do is "kill 'em with kindness." My favorite saying is that you get more with honey than with vinegar. Once you're nice to people, kind to people, you can establish a common ground. Just because you don't agree with each other doesn't mean there isn't some common ground. I also look for the good in people. I may not agree with what they're saying, but they always have good qualities.

JANET BR AY ATTWOOD: Have you ever tried looking at your adver- sity as if it were the best thing that could have happened to you? Have you noticed that there might have been some good in that? If not, you may want to play the "appreciation game." This is a game in which you start looking at what you *did* do right, instead of what you *didn't* do right. Whatever you put your attention on grows stronger in your life. So what kind of habit do you want to develop? Do you really want to develop a habit in which you're always looking at all the things that are working against you?

NIURKA: When I see someone as an adversary, I realize that they're trig- gering something in me that needs healing. People don't push your but- tons; they reflect yourself back to you. So I ask myself what I can learn in the situation, and I separate the behavior from the person. I look into the essence of the person's being and say, "Namaste! The divine in me recognizes the divine in you." I recognize that the same life force that's causing that person's heart to beat at this moment is the same life force that's causing my heart to beat. And then I ask myself the question, "How can I elevate my frequency, raise my level of awareness and energy to connect in a way that matches this other person?"

JOHN CAS TAGNINI: Here are a few action steps you can take: Think about a time in your life when you didn't think the experience was per- fect. Were you aware of the Gift in that experience? Where was the Gift physically? Where was it financially? Who did you get closer with? What was your union with the divine from this experience? Who did you gain a relationship with? What were the lessons you learned from it? How did it serve you? How did it serve other people? It's really about asking better questions. To get to the place where you see that experience as a Gift, sit down, take out your journal, and ask the question, "What were the Gifts?" By answering the question, you will get to the point of self- awareness and understanding, your presence.

One question to ask is "What is it I don't like about myself ?" Be as specific as you can in answering the question. And then ask yourself, "How has this thing been a Gift in my life? How has it served me? How has it served other people? How is it a blessing?" You need to get to the point where you can see that it was perfect the way it was, and that it's made you who you are today, and you are as perfect as anyone else on this planet.

MARY MANIN MORRISEY: The next time that something happens in your life that you're sure is bad, practice something called "pause power." Just push your internal pause button and then wait three days. During those three days, your assignment is to just stay in the question, "What possible good could be in this experience for me? What possible good could I find in this?"

GROWTH OPPORTUNITIES

Question Meditation

Think back to a major adversity in your life. As awful as it was, as you look back now, notice if you can see or find anything good that came out of it. Maybe it was a new friend. A job. Clarity. A new beginning. Write the event and its outcomes down in your journal, and express your emo- tions about the highs and the lows of that experience.

We want to be clear that finding the good in a bad situation does not negate the fact that something awful and bad happened in your life. These situations can create pain and fear in our emotions, our bodies, and our minds. We empathize with your suffering. We've been there too and understand how difficult it can sometimes be to deal with these situations. However, if we are willing to move through our pain and our fear—and by moving through, we mean acknowledging our feelings honestly and courageously and allowing them to exist and to be given a voice—adversity displays Gifts, whether we are aware of them or not.

Take a deep breath, and calm your mind. Now ask yourself the ques- tion, "What good came out of my adversity?" Take another breath and clear your mind. Ask yourself the question again: "What possible Gift exists there?"

Once you have thought of what possible Gift exists here, focus your mind on it. Pay attention to what starts to happen. You'll find that your mind starts to generate ideas not only about what Gift exists, but also about how to hone in on your Gifts. Write down the ideas as they come to you.

Shajen's "Who Am I?" Collage

This exercise is designed to help you create an authentic, positive vision for yourself. It will take approximately 60 minutes and is fun to do with friends and family.

First you will want to collect photos and magazines on your favorite topics, people, and interests. You can also use small items like shells, beads, favorite symbols, and the like. If you want to get really creative, your local thrift store or arts-and-crafts store should have lots of fun options for you.

This practice is one of my favorites and one that I have been using with my students, both young and old. I especially enjoy doing it during times of transition or when I am aware that I am going through a major evolutionary phase.

1. Begin by asking yourself the following question: "Who am I?"
2. Allow all and any thoughts that are positive to be noted; if negative thoughts appear, acknowledge them and let them go.
3. Again ask yourself the same question, "Who am I?" And also "Who do I want to be?"

4. Now ask yourself, "What Gifts are seeking to emerge and express themselves through me? What do I want to do? Who do I want to be?" And "How do I want to help?"

5. Write down all the ideas, feelings, pictures, tunes, and the like that come to you.

6. Begin to look through your magazines and photos. Cut out, in any shape you desire, the topics, people, and in- terests that light you up and inspire you. Personally, I like to use words a lot when I am making a collage.

7. After you have collected enough visuals, symbols, and words, begin making your collage and *have fun.*

8. When you are done, look at what you have made. Look at your choices, become aware of how those choices make you feel. Examine the ones that make you feel ex- cited and possibly a little nervous (in a good way).

9. Note in your journal any and all feelings and "aha" moments. Notice what Gifts inside you are trying to emerge, and write them down.

STEP 7: CREATING A CONSCIOUS AND COMPASSIONATE WORLD

Violet Mandala
Compassion = Violet Lotus Sparkles

•　　•　　•

Love and compassion are necessities, not luxuries. Without them humanity cannot survive.

— HIS HOLINESS THE DALAI LAMA

Step 7, creating a conscious and compassionate world, reminds us that, awestruck by life, the children are the future. Through discovering our own Gifts and by supporting the children to find theirs—to be their happiest and most joyous selves—we can create a world of peace and love. It is our deepest desire to create this world through personal de- velopment and lifelong learning. Facilitating the growth of others and helping them to find their path creates joy in our beings and, we strongly believe, in a world that supports a win for you, a win for me, and a win for all.

When we discover and open ourselves to who we are, it inspires oth- ers to do the same, and thus we all become active players in the planetary shift in consciousness toward a more compassionate world.

This ability to be open allows for compassion to emerge and grow. When we are able to be compassionate, we are able to forgive. It is vital to understand that forgiveness transforms the soul and unlocks your journey to your Gifts.

The way to a conscious, compassionate world is through our sons and daughters, brothers and sisters, nieces and nephews, friends and neighbors—-but in order to get the message to them, we have to model it ourselves first. So it starts with the self, by discovering who you really are, by discovering your true essence. When you start to emerge and ex- press yourself, you begin to be the ideal role model for yourself, for the people around you, and for the children.

Societies often work really hard to fit everyone into specific and molded ways of being. One goal of *Discover the Gift* is to open you to the possibility of creating a future for our children that provides the educa- tion and support they need to experience who *they* are at the core—and then show them how to shine from their core. We want them to express their Gifts without fear. The most important thing we can do is to help children to be in touch with who they really are, and ultimately allow them to be who they really are by teaching them what's right about them. As Bobbi DePorter says, "It's really special when kids get that they are the Gift. It just doesn't happen enough. Most of the time, they feel as if they have to prove themselves, or that there are expectations they can't live up to. So they feel the pressure. When they can take a step back, and take a breath, be themselves, and see how things can change around them, the stress disappears, they have more success in their lives, and they feel better about themselves. They participate more, they speak up more, and everything in their life changes.

"Buckminster Fuller, who has been called the Leonardo DaVinci of our time, and an authentic futurist, regarded the children as the future. Bucky was telling an audience about how to make the world work, and his ideas were going way over their heads. Then he saw a ten-year-old boy at the back of the room and asked him to come forward. He asked the child, 'Would you tell the audience what I just said?' and the boy repeated everything that Bucky had said, but in a way that everyone un- derstood. Bucky said that when he grew up, nobody asked his opinion. It was 'Never mind what you think!' Now children are expressing them- selves. Teenagers have profound things to say, and a thousand years from now we'll have a much better world for it."

A Compassionate World

We know more now about the world than we've ever known, but we sometimes seem to be doing less in the world. It's very interesting be- cause it's really important that we honor the earth and its inhabitants.

The earth itself is a being. And by living on the earth we are cocreators with it in life. We must respect it and leave it better than we found it.

As many spiritual cultures have said, we don't own the earth; we are simply caretakers for our children and their children.

Another cause for concern is the idea that the next generation of children might have a shorter life span than ours. What's going on? Is it the food we're eating? The technology we're producing? The fuels we mine and drill for? Or can the answers be found in the sometimes short supply of compassion?

To create a conscious and compassionate world, we must begin with the very dirt beneath our feet, beneath our cities. We must become aware of ourselves and present to our presence on the earth.

TRANSFORMATIONAL WISDOM

MICHAEL BERNARD BECKWITH: We are experiencing a new kind of evolution. It's called conscious and participatory evolution—meaning that right here and right now, at this second, beginning with our own life, we can change, we can shift, we can grow and become who we're meant to be. Nothing can determine our growth, our unfoldment, our happiness except for ourselves.

HIS HOLINESS SRI SRI R AVI SHANKAR: Commitment for a better society should arise within each one of us. Technology has made the globe into a village, and it is spirituality that will make it into a family. Spirituality will unite people of all cultures, religions, and races into a harmonious society, into a harmonious family. A sense of belongingness should come among all generations. I think without a sense of belonging we are in trouble.

With only technology in our hands, we will destroy ourselves.

NIURKA: It just takes one person's awakening to elevate the conscious- ness of a family. It just takes one person's awakening to elevate the consciousness of a company or of a community. The awakened con- sciousness has a ripple effect in the world.

HIS HOLINESS THE DALAI LAMA: The future, good or bad, entirely depends upon present behavior and present action.

SIR KEN ROBINSON: Ideas divide us, values isolate us, and concepts keep us apart. I believe the next invention in human understanding will be to reconcile these different cultural ways of seeing, in the interest of expressing a common humanity. We know it's there, and when these veils start to be torn away, people will see one another more clearly as com- mon beings with common purposes.

Consciousness has a range of meanings. In its simplest meaning, consciousness is what we lose when we fall asleep and what we gain when we wake up. It is the state of being awake. Simple, and yet the richest meaning.

When we talk about raising consciousness in a more philosophical sense, we're talking about people waking up and being alert to the situa- tions in which they find themselves. It's more than just open eyes; it's open minds. I believe that for a long time, particularly in Western cultures, we've been half awake and not aware of the realities we've created around us.

Since the eighteenth century, we've come to equate being conscious with a certain type of rationality. And it has been very important.

It has been the process that has underpinned the industrial and scientific revo- lutions. In the West, we believe that thinking means making distinctions and being logical.

Yet there are other equally respectable and in many ways more im- portant traditions of thought. You get connected through meditation, through Buddhism, through Asian cultures. Thinking isn't just seen as making distinctions; it's seen as seeing relationships and making con- nections and observing how things are intimately integrated rather than separate. It's not coincidental that we invented formal logic in the West and no system of formal logic in the East. In the East, thinking is much more about seeing oneness rather than separateness.

SHEILA R. MC KEITHEN: I've decided that I have no enemies. You can't be my enemy unless I make you one, and I won't make you one. You are a child of the universe, finding your way, and so am I. Gandhi was right when he said, "You must bring to the world what you want to see in the world." If I choose to see you as my enemy, I help produce enemies in the world, and I don't want to do that! I don't want to heap that upon the heads of future generations. I'd like to leave the planet a better place than I found it.

CHE RYL HUNTER: When I was nineteen, I was abducted, beaten, and repeatedly raped. In the midst of this experience, the most unusual thing happened. I felt a feeling of safety emerging. The logic seems crazy, but my thought was that if I could live through this, I could live through anything. I didn't know if my abductors would let me live, but I did know in a profound revelation—not like some lofty concept, but an actual experience—that I was not my body. So even if my body didn't make it out of there, I would still make it out of there. And in that mo- ment, the unthinkable act turned into this Gift that I held in my heart. And forever since, I have felt safe.

Years later, I met Demian through participating in his personal de- velopment courses. I realized that one of my Gifts would be to lead these workshops. So I was trained, started leading the workshops, and was very successful . . . until I realized that something was missing. It turned out what was missing was me. Me, who supposedly always felt safe. I'd kept myself back. Everyone was sharing their personal stories, but I was not. I knew my story about the abduction and beating and rape was a Gift, but it was my personal, private Gift. I hadn't told any- body about it, and I had no intention of doing so. I thought people would pity me or think I was a victim or think I was a fool for having gotten myself into that situation in the first place. I thought they might think I was unfit to lead the course because I had a far from perfect life myself.

Demian asked me, "Is this your calling?"

"Well, yes!" I said without question. "I come alive when I do this. Everybody else thinks so, as well." "Great," he said. "Then it's your Gift."

Two days later, I was back in the room, in front of hundreds of people. A woman stood up in the front of the room and was sharing that she was clear she could never move on after her divorce. The divorce had crushed her. And while I felt for her, my feelings for her made no difference because I hadn't shared my experience. So I did. In that mo- ment, life altered because each of us got that we are not defined by our circumstances.

We are not a function of our past, and there is no inherently good or bad event. Only our naming makes it so. A profound Gift of being alive is the ability to ask, "Is this a blessing, or is this a curse?" When we ask that question, life recontextualizes itself; in the moment I named my horrible experience as a Gift, my past was different. My present was most certainly distinct, and the future became a far different world than I had projected. It truly became a space where anything was possible.

DEMIAN LICHTENSTEIN: If everyone could take this journey discov- ering the Gift within their own being, then what kind of world would we have? If you and I are willing to engage in a consciously open con- versation about what is possible, then what is possible is *anything*. The world could be unified as one, like a global chorus singing all together. Are there problems in the world? You betcha! Is there war and hunger, famine, disease, pain, and sorrow? Absolutely. But even those are Gifts, the opportunity for all of us to raise our own awareness, to open our- selves to the possibility of universal love, and to engage in a true dis- covery of the Gift within our own souls and the Gift of the miracle of our life.

CHE RYL HUNTER: What if our only job is to walk through life con- sciously, choosing that which positively impacts our lives? Something to think about.

SIR KEN ROBINSON: You can't promote states of being that you your- self don't understand. You can't promote world peace if you are angry. As Gandhi said, "You must be the change you want to see in the world." Everything begins with your own transformation.

NIURKA: When you look at the essence of self-help and world help, you'll notice that these ideas are really one and the same. Our path is not about figuring out which one is more important. It's about bringing the two concepts together and realizing that all along they've been the same. What's beautiful is that science is illuminating what the spiritual masters have been saying for centuries: that we are in a universe of infinite possibilities; that you are a divine being; that we are one with all that is.

PERSONAL PRACTICES

HIS HOLINESS THE DALAI LAMA: One of the basic factors that de- velop mental disorder is a lack of affection and compassion. Human beings, you see, need compassion.

HIS HOLINESS SRI SRI R AVI SHANKAR: There is no point in ex- pressing our ideas to those who always agree with us. We have to get across to those who don't agree with us. That is where we are most needed. A doctor has no business in a healthy community. He has more jobs where people are sick. Opposite values are complementary. Where there is the need for peace, that is where the message of peace has to reach. And where there is distress, that is where compassion has a role to play. Where there is conflict, that is where cooperation is needed. The conviction within us will drive us to take up those challenges. Our conviction will allow us to venture into those areas we find hard or difficult.

JACK CANFIELD: One of the greatest Gifts you can give in relation- ships is listening. We all want to be listened to, but very few of us actually listen. When you listen completely to people, they get empty and they're ready to hear you, because they experience that someone's there to receive them. It's a simple Gift. It doesn't require more than maybe nodding, saying "uh-huh" and repeating back what you hear, and really being curious about wanting to hear what the other person's experience is.

CHRISTINE STEVENS: Stay present to that definite moment of sur- render when you just let go of your agenda and decide that you are here to serve.

CYNTHIA M. RUIZ: We can't change the past. It's sometimes impos- sible to resist trying, but it's simple to let go. Practice that.

STE WA RT EME RY: Swami Muktananda, an Indian master who has passed on, had a very simple teaching: "Welcome others with great re- spect and great love." I've noticed that if I choose to do that, I feel joyful. Why fear people just to protect ourselves? I understand that reaching out and welcoming others with respect and warmth may not be within the realm of awareness for some of us. I noticed that when I started doing it, I felt awkward, because I'd never been that way before. But as I started to learn to reach out, and make it a practice, I got better at it and found I was more joyful.

GROWTH OPPORTUNITIES

Ask, Listen, Act

Grab your discovery journal and take a few moments to settle your mind and body into a comfortable and relaxed place. Now, listen to what you are thinking and feeling at this moment. What's going on? Are you wor- ried about bills? Or a loved one who may be sick? Are you thinking about the future? A trip? A new job? Your destiny?! Are you thinking about the possibilities of your future? Just become conscious of what's going on inside you. What is your inner guidance saying? Just listen and don't worry about the "how to get there" of any possibility. Allow all pos- sibilities to exist. Ask yourself the following questions and when you're ready, record your responses in your discovery journal:

- Which actions, thoughts, and feelings will ultimately bring me to a feeling of compassion and peace along my journey to discovering my Gift?
- What changes would I have to make right now to begin expressing this compassion? Would I have to forgive someone? Become an activist? Stand up for someone who needs my help?
- Would I indeed make those changes? If not, what is hold- ing me back?
- Examine your reasons for changing or not changing. Would a change bring about peace? Is there something you can do to move closer to that experience?
- How well do I listen to others? How can I improve? How can I be present to those around me?
- Practice listening to those around you. The way to really listen is to first become present and aware of yourself. That way, when you are practicing listening, you will no- tice when you stop listening to others and begin focusing on yourself again.

Take time to write down all thoughts, feelings, visions, and the like.

There are no correct answers. There are no best answers. There is only what you hear back from yourself. Be with that, and acknowledge that. Sometimes we are ready to grow quickly and are inspired to become something new. And sometimes we grow by simply realizing that we are afraid to, and this realization allows us to step through our fear.

Being of service connects you to the world. When you give peace to oth- ers, more of what you desire comes to you. In this exercise, think of one way in which you can bring about peace by utilizing one of your Gifts. Search yourself and find what is most true for you.

Now that you have inner-acted—gone into yourself to find one of your Gifts—try interacting by giving your Gift freely. Maybe it's a poem you've written that will bring someone a feeling of love. Maybe it's a song you can sing that will remind someone of forgiveness. Maybe it's a word of advice that will remind another of compassion. Whatever your heart reveals to you, give it away. You know, compassion and peace are two things that, when given away, make you richer in every part of your life.

"Hands of Peace" Meditation

Imagine before you two outstretched hands. The palms are up, and the hands come together as if they are cupping falling water. Hold that image in your mind until it becomes very clear. These are big, strong, powerful hands.

Consider another image. With your eyes still closed, think of a prob- lem in your life, something you've been worrying about but over which you have absolutely no control. Maybe you're late on your rent. Maybe a relative is sick. Maybe you are angry at a friend. Whatever it is, picture the problem in your mind.

Now take that image, that problem, that thing you've been worrying about, and place it in the open hands. How do you do that? You can imagine the problem as if it's a snapshot, a photograph, or a still life and repeat these words: "I place my problems in the hands of peace and have faith that love and compassion will transform this worry into harmony and tranquility."

Allow yourself to experience the feeling of calm that the hands of peace bring you.

STEP 8: LOVE—THE ULTIMATE GIFT

The Unified Field
Unity = White Lotus with Colored Sparkles

•　　•　　•

All the major world religions are emphasizing the importance of love and compassion, and love and forgiveness.

— HIS HOLINESS THE DALAI LAMA

Step 8, love, is why we are here.

There is no other reason for our existence other than to experience love and to share it with the rest of the world. Love gives us the power to forgive even that which we perceive as unforgivable. It grants the ability to be grateful for our very existence. The attitude of gratitude creates the state of grace.

Love brings us together in unity.

Unity helps us to understand that we live in a world where everything is connected to everything else. Everything we do, say, think, and believe affects others and the universe around us. It's like what happens when all the colors of the rainbow come together as one. We get the most beauti- ful and powerful white light.

The Unity of Love

Love enables you to go out into the world and share your Gift, and to help other people to discover theirs. You are now able to spread your power and give love, receive love, be in gratitude, and have powerful and clear intentions.

Love is the highest vibration we reach. It is total harmony, the ulti- mate Gift. It is pure and authentic in its ability to heal and transform. At this stage, we can only see others as our brothers and sisters. We can see the perfection of the universe and experience its infinite love. It is ever-present, awaiting our arrival.

Universal love sustains us all, and we are all meant to be pathfinders on a great journey toward fully tapping into love and helping others do the same.

If we all could take this journey of transformation, this journey of discovering the Gifts within ourselves and sharing those Gifts, just imag- ine what kind of world we would have. If we are willing to engage in a conscious and open conversation about what is possible, then that will- ingness itself means that anything is possible.

If we saw the world as a unified global chorus singing together, would there still be problems in the world? Probably. Would there be war, hun- ger, famine, disease, pain, and sorrow? Perhaps. But as Step 6, adversity, posits, even those are opportunities for all of us to raise our own aware- ness, to open ourselves to the possibility of universal love, to engage in a true discovery of our Gifts, and the Gift of the miracle of our life in furtherance of a conscious and compassionate world.

This ultimate Gift is the essence of who we are as individuals. More than anything, we want to connect, to feel whole, to love and be loved. We have found that the best way to go about life is with an open heart. Everyone deserves love.

Have you ever had a newborn infant or baby placed into your hands? In that moment you get that it's all about love. You are holding love in your hands. This tiny being cannot survive without nurturing, and com- passion. You begin to understand that every being comes into this world the same way, open to love.

Sharing who you are—a person filled with love and compassion—is the essence of sharing your Gift.

Teaching love, acting with love, feeling our hearts full of love—all this sets off an incredible chain reaction whose effects are magnified a thousand times for every person who becomes a pathfinder on the journey. We support each other, raise happy children, sustain and build the Gift every day, every year, every generation. When parents treat their children with kindness and respect, these children can grow up to treat their children with kindness and respect—and so on. Love is amplified over time, because the person who creates a happier family creates a happier community, creates a happier world of compassion in which all children have possibility, a world in which everyone has the right to shine, and everyone's voice counts.

As idealistic as that is, we believe it's also possible. It's why we're here.

TRANSFORMATIONAL WISDOM

JACK CANFIELD: What we're really doing in any situation is bringing the quality of our being—love, joy, peace, compassion, happiness, and justice—to all of humanity. When we're loving, we create an inclusive vibration. We may say words like "I love you," but what we're really ex- pressing is the vibration. We know from communication theory that the actual words we say are a very small part of the communication. It's the quality of the energy—the enthusiasm or lack of it, the love or the lack of it, the anger or the lack of it—that really has the most impact.

TER RY TILLMAN: There's nothing that loving won't heal. Nothing. I get that. I also forget that sometimes. But I never forget that I've gotten it, and I know I can return there. When I do, my life is beautiful, and the results I produce are positive; it kind of spills over, and someone else picks it up and passes it on, and it just multiplies that way.

MICHAEL BERNARD BECKWITH: "Agape" means unconditional love. It's a Greek word. Dr. Martin Luther King Jr. described it as "the love of God operating in the human heart." The love without condi- tion, the love without agenda, not based on merit or demerit. It's a love that cannot be done with the mind. It's a love that takes us over when our heart is open and we discover there's no boundary between us, that you are a dimension of me and I am a dimension of you. That we are really one.

When we rise to love at that level, through spiritual practice and in- tentionality, we begin to live in a different world. That is, we remove the filters and the inhibitions so that love can take over our life and impel us into right action. As human beings, we fall forward; we stumble forward, doing the best that we can. In the process of becoming, we perfect our love along the way, becoming better at it, year after year, through the practice of these sacred truths.

Love has the final word. It wears down every seeming opponent. A person may even hate you, but if you do not engage in that vibration and you continue to love anyway, love is more powerful than hate. And even- tually it works its way into that person's heart and change occurs.

SHEILA R. MCKEITHEN: I once heard this story: Love, Wealth, and Success knocked on a door, and two grandparents answered. "Come on in!" they said. But the three visitors said, "We can't all come in. You can only invite one of us in."

"Love, Wealth, Success: who do I invite in?" the grandfather asked the grandmother. But before she could say anything, their little grand- daughter answered. "Invite Love in!" she shouted. They did, and when Love walked in, the other two followed. Grandpa exclaimed, "But you said only one of you could come in!" And Love responded, "Where I go, they follow me."

BILL HARRIS: The people known historically for having the greatest amount of inner peace are those who finally realize that the sepa- rate self they thought they were was actually only a conceptualization.

The most amazing thing happens when you actually realize that. I don't mean knowing it theoretically or intellectually, but actually *experiencing* having no boundaries, experiencing that you are connected to one vast, interconnected everything. Once that happens, you feel the side effect: Since you are everywhere, there's nowhere to go. Since you're everything, there's nothing outside of you that can threaten you. An intense peace follows. People who have had this experience know that they can now *play* at being a separate self, but that they are not separate.

HIS HOLINESS SRI SRI R AVI SHANKAR: Often a situation calls for a response. Instead, we *react*. When we react, we lose sight of our- selves, our inner strength. It is vital for us to *respond,* keeping who we are and what we are in view. We must take one step at a time with alertness. That makes all the difference.

In the big picture, when we recognize that we are global beings and that the whole world is our family, the world will be less corrupt. Re- ligion will be free from fanaticism and terrorism. Politics will be free from greed and cunningness. Business will be more ethical and will have corporate and social responsibility.

TER RY COLE- WHITTAKER: There's only one religion, and that reli- gion is love. The love of God. God is all-inclusive. This means that as I love God, I love you because you're part of God. I love every animal and every plant because they are also God.

RICK MARS: My wife was the ultimate Gift for me. She passed away recently. So, in gratitude to her for filling my life with so much love, I would like to share this message:

"Sweetheart, I accept full responsibility for the Gifts you gave me and the paths to new Gifts that you led me on. And I promise for the rest of my life I will honor and respect the woman who so graciously chose to fill my life and who taught me the true meaning of joy.

"I love you, and your children love you.

"I can feel your spirit every day through the Gifts that you left me. You left a legacy that is much bigger than I ever knew. At your event the other night, two cameras were running. I didn't realize that one of them was live-streaming the entire event globally, but afterward I got e-mails from China, Malaysia, New Zealand, Australia, England, all over the world. Groups of people actually got together to watch those who loved you celebrate your life.

"I miss you terribly. And I will live up to your standards. I love you." As people look back a thousand years from now, my hope is that humanity will have learned just that—that we are humanity. We are not separate. We are connected. We are all part of each other. We try not to be. We work very hard at not being. We love to put up boundaries. We love to build political differences, religious differences. But I think what is maybe beginning is that we are all looking for the Gift in one another. It's so simple. All it takes is to realize that there is only love.

There is only love.

TER RY TILLMAN: It's a key principle of the self-help/human potential movement that we are connected at a deeper level. We connect through the essence of the soul, and we connect to that essence through loving, through compassion, through understanding, through kindness, through caring, through peace, through joy.

We can create those experiences of connection inside of us. All those qualities are already inside of us—we didn't get them from somewhere outside of us. It wasn't the new car, more money, a longer vacation, or new clothes that gave it to us, because if that were the case, every time I put on new clothes, I'd be joyful. But that's not the case. I buy that new suit. I feel great the first time I wear it and pretty good the next time, but by the fourth time, it's just another piece of clothing. The feeling "great" and "confident" wasn't in the clothes. It was within me.

JOE VI TALE: The ultimate Gift I can give to a person or to the world is love. By love I mean acceptance. Too many people feel they are not accepted—let alone loved. Another way of saying it is that they feel judged. We don't have to judge people. We simply need to accept them for who they are, what they are, what they want to do. If we did that with everyone, there would be no reasons for violence or war or conflict, because the love would be there, the peace would be, and the nonjudg- mentalness would transform us all.

SHEILA R. MC KEITHEN: There is really only one law: the law of love. Not love as an emotion, because love is not an emotion. Love works through the emotions. Love is oneness. When you come from love, peo- ple get it. You apply your Gift because you want to live in integrity. In the end, that's all you've got. No one on their deathbed asks for a Rolls-Royce. Or a million dollars. Or a bigger home to die in! I will ask for love and compassion.

CYNTHIA M. RUIZ: So many people in love try to control the other person. But love isn't controlling. It's unconditional. That means we ac- cept others. It doesn't mean we'll always agree with them, or that they're perfect and don't make mistakes. Love is working through those mis- takes, apologizing, forgiving, and moving on.

SHAJEN JOY AZIZ: Once, when I asked my husband what he thought my Gift is, he smiled so grandly that my stomach rippled with excitement.

He looked at me with such love in his eyes and said, "Your compas- sion and empathy, your ability to feel with others and help them move through their hard times with a positive spirit amazes me. It is one of the things I treasure in you so dearly."

These words from my husband almost ten years into our relationship created the most beautiful energy for both of us and continues to do so today.

CHRISTINE STEVENS: The experience that most transformed my heart was working in Iraq and making music with people I had thought were my enemies. I found we shared a love that didn't need language. I never knew people's names, and I never spoke to them. I couldn't say hello or good-bye. We never even counted music together. We just started to connect through the drum, through rhythm, through the simple, simple act of drumming together. As a parting gift, I was given a large frame drum called a *daf.* Written on my drum in Farsi is this: "There is no greater sound than love, the vibration that encircles the universe forever."

A common pulse unites humanity. We are all walking, talking poly- rhythms, and when we drum together, it changes our relationships be- cause we remember our common rhythm, our oneness. In drumming, we call the downbeat the "one," so when we fall into the groove together, we actually experience oneness. We don't think about it, talk about it; there are no words. Instead, we move out of the mind and find our common heartbeat.

PERSONAL PRACTICES

SHEILA R. MC KEITHEN: Practice loving yourself. Give yourself per- mission to live your dreams. Give yourself permission to be well. Give yourself permission to be forgiven for past mistakes. Give yourself per- mission to start over. All these are acts of love.

MA RY MANIN MORRISEY: I begin my morning meditation with "I am so happy and grateful to be given a brand-new baby day." Gratitude is the great multiplier. When we think from gratitude, we see more, we feel more, we're available to more, and we also can sense what some call the voice of intuition. Others call it the voice for God, the still, small voice, or, as Gandhi called it, "the voice for truth." All I know is that this is the way I want to live my life, every day.

CHRISTINE STEVENS: "The more you give, the more you get." Repeat that three times, if you will.

"So give your heart away." Repeat that three times.

"The more you give, the more you get." Repeat. "So give your love away."

MICHAEL BERNARD BECKWITH: Ultimately, love is the first word, and it is the final word. It is the alpha and the omega.

Since love and compassion and forgiveness are common to the world religions, it is imperative that we find ways to practice being open. So: Sit in your room alone and be loving; radiate it, emanate it, fill the whole room with your love energy. Immerse yourself in the vibration—feel it, visualize it, create vibrations of love energy around you.

Visualize yourself sending out a massive shock wave, almost like a sonic boom that shoots out across your room. Immediately you'll feel that something is happening, like a warmth arising in and around your body. Be present to what you're feeling. Allow yourself to soak in the experience. Bring this energy with you throughout your day and pay attention to how people react to you. You'll see how they react to your energy.

BARBARA DE ANGELIS: All we have to do is examine nature to see the one truth: everything is always changing. Nothing is stationary. Even at this moment your body is changing. Cells are dying and growing as you read this wonderful book. You're not the same right now as you were even a minute ago. Change is the law underneath everything. Change is the wonderful ride we are all on, and if we can partner with it instead of feeling it's ruined our plans or trying to control it, we can be in tune with the law of the universe expanding us toward more and more majesty, and mystery, and bliss.

SONIA POWERS: I try to think of this time as that moment in history when people became conscious and chose to be responsible. They chose to look at what was happening in their lives as a Gift. They chose to express their own Gifts. They chose to be that which they were seeking. And in seeking and being, they shared their Gifts with other people. We let go of war, and we let go of sickness, we discovered that there was enough of everything, that all we needed was to be ourselves, and that would be enough.

CYNTHIA M. RUIZ: We all have and make choices every day. The way I convey this to my employees is through a program called Value-Driven Leadership. It means that you lead by example and respect. You respect others, you respect yourself, and at the end of the day, when you make the tough decisions, they're based on your core values. If you stick to your core values, you'll never make a wrong choice. You may not make everybody happy, but you'll make the right choice for you.

STEWART EME RY: I have a lot of joy in my life. Sometimes it's over- whelming. But I can't tell you why, because I subscribe to the notion of being happy for no reason. This I know: no one is joyful and fearful at the same time, so it has something to do with the absence of fear.

HIS HOLINESS THE DALAI LAMA: There is no need for temples, no need for complicated philosophy. Our own brain, our own heart, is our temple. The philosophy is kindness. This is my simple religion.

I feel that compassion is not merely a "warm heart." I think that with genuine compassion, there is a sense of responsibility. That's why I'm always trying to share my own experience. Whether they accept it or not is a different matter. But I do feel that if I explain some- thing according to my experience, at least some people might get some new ideas.

SHAJEN JOY AZIZ: We all have different levels of self-doubt, fear, and things that prevent us from moving forward in life. But one of the things I've learned doing this project, *Discover the Gift,* was how to step through my fears, how to move through those obstacles that I had inside. And the hardest thing to do is to just do it.

Love is everywhere around us. Now it's time to ask this question: If everyone could take this journey of discovering the Gift within their own being, and sharing that Gift throughout the world, what kind of people would they be? What kind of person do *you* want to be? What kind of world do you want?

GROWTH OPPO RTUNITIES

Practice Love

1. Give yourself permission to love yourself.
2. Give yourself permission to live your dreams.
3. Give yourself permission to be well.
4. Give yourself permission to be forgiven for past mis- takes.
5. Give yourself permission to start over. All of these are acts of love.

Appreciation and Gratitude Meditation

This meditation generates deep appreciation and gratitude for yourself and our world.

Start by finding a comfortable place to sit and calm your breathing.

Next, develop gratitude for the seat you are sitting on. Thank it for supporting you. Then show gratitude for the person who made the seat and for anyone who might have been involved in the process.

Next, expand your gratitude to the building you are in. Give appre- ciation and thanks for the protection and safety it provides and for the space it is giving you. Show appreciation to the people who built it and all the materials used in the process.

Now begin to give gratitude to the earth beneath you. Show love and appreciation toward the earth, for it maintains and supports life. Appre- ciate all living things—plants and trees, birds and animals, marine life. They are all integrated parts of the whole.

Bring your appreciation to your body. Feel gratitude toward yourself for the way your body supports and nourishes you, how it enables you to feel love, happiness, and joy. Be present to the energy moving through your body. Acknowledge how your being is connected to the earth, from the food you eat and the water you drink to the air that you breathe. Show gratitude and appreciation for the connection your physical body has to all elements of life.

Next, send gratitude to your parents. If it wasn't for them, you would not be walking this physical plane. Show appreciation for what they were able to give you and how they influenced and shaped you. Now expand your gratitude and appreciation toward your grandparents for them pass- ing on their wisdom and knowledge. Appreciate that they have returned back to the earth.

Now expand your gratitude and appreciation to include all beings. Be present to how we are all our own separate entities but all walk this earth together and breathe the same air.

Now bring your appreciation to your breath. Be present to the flow of the air as it enters and leaves your body. Remember that we do not own the air that we breathe; we share it. Show appreciation for the air we breathe, because it gives us life.

Finally, when you are ready, take a deep breath and gently stretch. Now bring your appreciation with you into your daily life and go out and love everything.

Mandalas: The Unified Field of Love Meditation

As we begin drawing to a close, we'd like to offer you this breathing meditation that summarizes everything we've learned so far and will help you become aware of and experience each of the steps contained in *Dis- cover the Gift*. This is an active meditation that uses deep, rapid breathing as well as body movement to open and bring awareness to eight energy centers, the chakras, each of which is represented in each chapter and in the insert by a specific colored mandala. We suggest you return to pages 72–73 to review the chakras and their corresponding mandalas, and turn to the color mandala insert while you do this exercise.

This meditation is best done on an empty stomach, either early in the morning or in the evening before dinner. For the first step, stand with your feet about as wide apart as your hips, let your body become loose and relaxed. Close your eyes, open your mouth slightly, and begin to breathe deeply and rapidly into the first chakra, represented by the red mandala. Your breath in and out should last about one second. This is the place of receptivity, a place of openness and stability. As you breathe, let your attention fall to your pelvic area. Keep equal emphasis on your breath moving in and out, and breathe in a rhythm that feels comfortable to you—don't force it.

Breathe into the first chakra, located at the base of your spine, for about a minute or two, meditating on receptivity and what you've learned along your journey about flexibility. You don't have to think hard. Just allow your thoughts and messages from your intuition to come naturally.

Then move your breathing into the second chakra, represented by the or- ange mandala, the center of intention, located at your navel level. Repeat the process as noted above, focusing your attentive breath on the power of intending a life filled with possibilities. Keep moving your deep, rapid breathing up into the third chakra, represented by the yellow mandala, and which is a place of power and action. Allow your attention to rest here and feel your inner strength rising up inside you. Stay here for a few moments and then gradually and naturally move your focus to the fourth chakra, represented by the green mandala. Breathe in, and as you exhale, allow the stability, creativity, and power from your first three chakras to rise and fill your heart. Stay here for a few moments and then shift your focus to the fifth chakra, the area of the throat, symbolized by the blue mandala. This is the center of our communications. Again, allow all the energy from the chakras below this one to energize your inner voice, which, in turn, will stimulate your outer voice in the way you express yourself.

Now shift your focus to the sixth chakra—the indigo mandala—what many people call the third eye, and is the center of our intuition and true vision. Allow your breathing to cleanse and energize this area. Working on your sixth chakra will make you more aware of yourself and the world around you. And the more we understand our inner and outer realities, the more we are able to activate the Gift that is inside us.

From here, gradually shift your attention to the seventh chakra, or the crown, which is located at the top of your head, and is represented by the violet mandala. Allow your deep breathing to rise from your root chakra all the way up the ladder of your being, into and through your crown. As it bursts forth, allow the energy to surround and protect you.

You'll notice that by the time you get to the eighth center, love, that it's not a center at all, but a unified field of experience, a grand white light that surrounds and connects all of the steps, centers, mandalas, people, and worlds together. Here is an overview of the steps, their as- sociated mandalas, and their corresponding chakras:

- Receptivity: Red Mandala—Root Chakra
- Intention: Orange Mandala—Second Chakra
- Activation: Yellow Mandala—Third Chakra
- Infinite Feedback: Green Mandala—Fourth Chakra
- Vibration: Blue Mandala—Fifth Chakra
- Adversity and Transformation: Indigo Mandala—Sixth Chakra
- Creating a Conscious and Compassionate World: Violet Mandala—Seventh Chakra
- Love: The Unified Field

As you breathe up from chakra to chakra, your breathing should be- come more rapid, but gentle, so that you are taking twice as many breaths in the eighth chakra as you were in the first.

While you practice this meditation, it is helpful to shake your body, stretch, tilt and rotate your pelvis, and move your hands in any way that you want, but keep your feet planted in the same position. Keep your awareness with the sensation of the chakras, as opposed to your breath- ing and body movement.

Once you have been breathing in the eighth chakra for a while, let your breath, awareness, and love turn and fall back down through each chakra, and let your breath slow down as you move from one to the next. Let love permeate all of your being.

This process should take about two minutes, although it's up to you to decide how long you breathe into each chakra. When you have fin- ished the sequence, stand silently for a bit, then start the sequence again. This upward and downward breathing sequence can be repeated three or more times.

If at first you don't feel the energy of your chakras, just breathe into the place where they are located in your body. Bring love to those areas. Remember not to push the breath, but just allow it to flow through you and carry you into the sensations and qualities of each chakra. The more you let love energize your body, mind, and soul, the more your Gift will reveal itself to you.

FOLLOW YOUR HEART

•　　•　　•

Because of Demian's transformation, we are now all members of a family fully wrapped in unconditional love and support. We continually experi- ence ourselves as more connected to each other, to our family, others, and to the universe.

The discovery of our Gifts has resulted in our hearts healing and the ultimate Gift of love. We are now the beings we've always wanted to be with each other, our families, our friends, in business, and in our com- munity. Living life is like sailing. You're constantly making adjustments and corrections, but once you take the wheel and set your course, you can go anywhere. And after this long journey, if there is any wisdom we can offer, it is simply this: follow your heart, discover your Gift, and get ready for the greatest adventure of your life.

Recognizing the precious, never-to-be-repeated Gift of both your existence and our existence, we have offered the path set forward in this book with the pure intention that it will be beneficial for all.

We really believe, as Mary Mannin Morrissey suggests, that "our soul speaks to us of its next expression through signals that come to our conscious mind." They are longing to be expressed. Even our discontent and blocks to our creativity want to be expressed. We are so much more than we've known, and we're so much more than we ever thought. This life is about the discovery and the delivery of that greatness.

That's why, in the process of putting our experiences and those of our family into both a book and a motion picture, it was necessary to explain the eight steps to discovering and unfolding your Gift. Some people call them by other names: steps, principles, distinctions, or communications. Whatever they're called, they are doorways to self-discovery, steps to the greatest Gift of all, love.

As His Holiness the Dalai Lama says, "The ultimate creator is the human mind." In order to begin to discover your Gifts, you must pay special attention to your internal thoughts and energy, and especially your heart, your inner wisdom and voice. Allow yourself to be guided by the heart instead of your rational mind.

The result is unity, and gratitude.

Being grateful is one of life's biggest treats. When you exist in a state of appreciation, it creates positive waves of energy and sends vibrations into the universe to touch others with your authenticity. When we ac- knowledge and appreciate others, ourselves, our paths and journey, we ignite a flame that never dies.

Our goal with *Discover the Gift* is to fan that flame. We know, through experience, that when we discover our Gifts, we create a life—and a world—filled with joy, fulfillment, abundance, leadership, and love. It's a win for me, a win for you, and a win for others. As we've seen on our journey together, the eight core steps facilitate a deeply powerful yet simple approach for you to:

- Open your heart.
- Reconnect with your true essence.
- Address fears that stop you from moving forward.
- Recondition your mind and emotions, replacing old lim- iting patterns and beliefs with positive thoughts, feelings, and behaviors.
- Discover your Gift through acknowledging your passions.

- Share your Gifts and be of service.
- Create fulfillment, joy, and connectedness for yourself and those around you through sharing what you enjoy most.
- Discover the Gift in all circumstances, no matter how adverse.
- Get rid of negative thought patterns, habits, and beliefs.
- Become a positive thinker and an active player in the game of your life.
- Forgive yourself and others because it transforms your soul.
- Rediscover your relationship to energy and understand how everything is energy.
- Become present to your presence on this earth.

We have come to learn that for us there are Gifts in all circumstances. Ultimately all is a Gift: your life, consciousness, love, and all the people in your life are the true Gifts. Two years ago, neither of us could have guessed that we'd be writing this; we couldn't have imagined our lives as they are now. We are here because step by step we moved through our fears and acknowledged our responsibilities.

We ask you to prevail in the face of your fears, to step through them, and to allow yourselves the freedom to be who you are so that others may be inspired to do the same. Stepping through our fears brings out possibilities we could never have foreseen—which makes sense, because we don't know yet what those possibilities are.

Our intention with *Discover the Gift* is to support the unfoldment of meaning in people's lives in hopes that the discovery of their true essence and their true Gifts will create abundance not only for them, but also for those around them.

Just the process of creating our book and movie brought up many questions, considerations, speculations, and fears. No one can know the future in the present. The only option was to forge ahead, to summon our already existing Gifts of storytelling and educating. We had to stop worrying about what anyone else thought and just do it because *that was the only way to get the answer.*

Understanding the unifying principles at the heart of the Gift of love helps us to see the web of connections that exist everywhere in our world, linking everyone and everything together. Anything we do, say, think, and believe affects us as individuals, as well as the universe. It is our profoundest wish that all people discover their Gifts and that they share them openly with a loving heart. The old paradigm of division and conflict is now giving way to a new world of sharing and growth. We are evolving, as always, but in a new, conscious, and participatory way.

This journey of discovery continues to unfold into higher and higher stages of alignment as the universe feeds back to us exactly what we share.

There's an old saying that states, "You do not describe what you see; you see what you describe." Thus it is our job to first describe the world we want to live in. This means to have a vision and to articulate it. Just as Layna Mawson, founder of the Orkidz Art Studio, shared with us in our film version of *Discover the Gift*, "Your art never has to be perfect." We ourselves feel this exact way: Life is not perfect, and your art doesn't have to be either. We are all "a work in progress," and this fact is yet another grand Gift. This means we need to be patient and flexible and know that each step—including the potholes and pitfalls—is part of the journey. In other words, we never, ever should feel the need to invalidate where we have been, because it has brought us here to this moment.

At the end of this process of creating *Discover the Gift*, we have found a place of serenity and forgiveness in our hearts. May you find the com- passion, peace, and love that we all seek. May your lives be an expression of joy and may all your dreams manifest to their fullest potential.

So share wisely.

After all, what kind of world do you want? Discover your Gift. It's why we're here.

Humbly, gratefully,
Shajen and Demian

FATHER GREG APPARCEL, CSP

Father Greg Apparcel is the 11th Rector of the Church of Santa Susanna in Rome. He has worked at Paulist Productions, the film and television unit of the Paulist Fathers, where he assisted in the research, marketing, and making of religious films and documentaries for television.

JANET BRAY ATTWOOD

A much-sought-after international inspirational speaker, Janet Bray Attwood is the coauthor of the *New York Times* bestseller *The Passion Test: The Effortless Path to Discovering Your Life Purpose,* and coauthor of *From Sad to Glad: 7 Steps to Facing Change with Love and Power.*

CHERIF AZIZ

Cherif Aziz, a founding member of ATL, the Association of Transformational Leaders, is the coproducer of *Discover the Gift* and senior vice president at Equilibrium Entertainment. His guiding principle is "busi- ness with integrity," and he prides himself on having clear and open communication for a smooth-running business creating win/win/win opportunities for all involved.

SHAJEN JOY AZIZ, M.ED.

Shajen Joy Aziz is the coauthor and executive producer of *Discover the Gift;* she is also director of operations at Equilibrium Entertainment.

A found- ing member of the Southern California Association of Transformational Leaders, Shajen Joy Aziz is passionate about children and young adults: they are our future. Her motto is "Learning for Life—Empowering the Future."

MICHAEL BERNARD BECKWITH

Teacher, author, broadcast personality, thought leader Michael Bernard Beckwith's life is a testament to building spiritual community. Gifted with a vision of a transdenominational spiritual community, he is the founder of the Agape International Spiritual Center in California.

JACK CANFIELD, M.ED.

Jack Canfield is an internationally recognized inspirational speaker, au- thor, and trainer. He is widely known as the coauthor of the bestselling *Chicken Soup for the Soul* series, with more than 200 titles and 115 million copies in print in forty-seven languages.

JOHN CASTAGNINI

John Castagnini is a human behavioral specialist, bestselling author, and respected founder of Thank God I . . ., a series of books, seminars, and a vibrant online community. He is a sought-after authority on the cor- relation between human emotion and universal principles.

TER RY COLE- WHITTAKER

Through the company she founded, Success Plus, Terry Cole-Whittaker is one of the first thought leaders to conduct human potential seminars for corporate America and Fortune 500 companies. She is a successful motivational and inspirational speaker who has authored five books and holds three honorary doctoral degrees.

SYDNEY CRESCI

Sydney Cresci is a multilingual expert in world travel and the founder of Make a Change Personal Discovery Journeys. Her "citizen of the world" approach to travel accounts for twenty-five years of success managing elaborate and enlightening journeys across the globe.

HIS HOLINESS THE DALAI LAMA

His Holiness the 14th Dalai Lama Tenzin Gyatso is both the head of state and the spiritual leader of Tibet.

BARBARA DE ANGELIS, PH.D.

Barbara De Angelis is one of the most influential teachers of our time in the field of relationships and personal growth. As a number one bestsell- ing author, popular television personality, and sought-after motivational speaker, she has been a pioneer in the field of personal transformation.

LUCIA DE GARCIA

Lucia De Garcia, a businessperson, laureate author, and inspirational speaker, is the founder of Élan International. Élan assists both foreign and domestic enterprises in Latin American business practices, opening new markets and expanding market share throughout the hemisphere.

ROBERTA "BOBBI" DEPORTER

Roberta "Bobbi" DePorter is president of the Quantum Learning Network (QLN), which produces Quantum Learning and SuperCamp programs for students, teachers, schools, and organizations across the United States as well as in Asia, Europe, and Latin America. She is also the author of more than a dozen books.

STEWA RT EME RY

Stewart Emery is an entrepreneur, an executive coach, and the bestselling author of *You Don't Have to Rehearse to Be Yourself* and *Do You Matter?* He is consistently identified as one of the ten most influential people in the human potential movement.

RITA GUEDES

Rita Guedes is a Brazilian actress famous for her role on the telenovela *Despedida de Solteiro* (*The Bachelor Party*), among others. She has also ap- peared in the shows *Carga Pesada* (*Heavy Load*) and *Vôce Decide* (*You Decide*).

MARK VICTOR HANSEN

Focused solely on helping people from all walks of life to reshape their vi- sion of what's possible, no one is better respected in the area of human po- tential than Mark Victor Hansen. Creating powerful change in thousands of organizations and millions of individuals worldwide for over thirty years, he delivers proven messages of possibility, opportunity, and action.

BILL HARRIS

Bill Harris, the president and director of Centerpointe Research Insti- tute, has been involved in personal development for more than thirty-five years as a seeker, teacher, public speaker, author, musician, composer, therapist, workshop leader, and business owner. He has studied and practiced a variety of traditional and modern transformational tech- niques and approaches.

PAUL HEUSSENSTAMM

Paul Heussenstamm is a unique artist, whose mandala paintings are fea- tured in the insert of this book. He has been sharing his unique Gift of helping people discover their soul through his own work and his "Art as a Spiritual Path" workshops worldwide.

CHE RYL HUNTER

Cheryl Hunter is a screenwriter, author, and transformational leader who merged two seemingly divergent careers around one idea: well-told stories that educate, entertain, and impact. She has led courses to 78,000 people, including at the University of California at Los Angeles, and has contracted with major movie studios and TV networks.

DEMIAN LICHTENSTEIN

Demian Lichtenstein is the coauthor, producer, and director of *Discover the Gift* and a globally recognized transformational leader. He has also di- rected major studio films such as *3000 Miles to Graceland* and music videos for Grammy-winning artists such as Sting and Eric Clapton. He currently serves on the Leadership Council of the Directors Guild of America and is the CEO of Equilibrium Entertainment, where he overseas all creative affairs, worldwide production, financing, and distribution.

JOHNNY MADONIA

Dedicated to the phenomenon of the "mind-body link," Johnny Madonia has advised, consulted, treated, and trained some of the world's most respected athletes, entertainers, and businesspeople. His ability to motivate is magnificent, and his ability to change one's thinking in an instant is uncanny.

RICK MARS

Reverend Rick Mars has produced, directed, and hosted the television shows *Health Ways, Community Focus,* and *Better Life TV.* He is a founding member of the Transformational Leadership Council, as well as a rever- end of the New Thought Church.

SHEILA R. MCKEITHEN, J.D.

Sheila R. McKeithen is currently the minister at the Universal Centre of Truth in Kingston, Jamaica, where she inspires people to live a more purposeful life. She is also the author of a monthly publication, *The Daily Inspiration,* and was formerly an assistant attorney general in Florida.

MA RY MANIN MORRISSEY

Speaker, bestselling author, and president and founder of LifeSOULutions, Mary Manin Morrissey is also the cofounder and first president of the Association for Global New Thought. With Michael Bernard Beckwith, she became the first New Thought minister to be appointed to the Executive Counsel of the Parliament of World Religions.

SUE MO RTER, D.C.

Sue Morter is a recognized authority on bridging science, spirit, and human possibility. Her high-energy presence in her many keynote ad- dresses, workshops, and programs ignites passion, imparts knowledge, and affects worldwide audiences of thousands.

NIURKA

Niurka is a transformational teacher and guide who inspires and empow- ers people to live powerfully, authentically, and purposefully. She is a dy- namic speaker, author, poet, and visionary whose work unites the world of business with the essential wisdom of mind-body-spirit.

PENNEY PEIRCE

Penney Peirce is a respected and gifted intuitive empath with deep psy- chological understanding, visionary ability, and business sense. She is one of the early pioneers in the intuition development movement.

SCOTT PETERSEN

Scott Petersen, the founder and director of the Refugio Altiplano, grew up in Michigan and took his first trip to South America at age seventeen to teach English in Ecuador and travel across the continent. He worked with Shipibo Indians and coastal shamans in Peru for seven years before discovering the ideal location for the exceptional healing center he estab- lished in 1996.

LYNN POMPEI

With the realization that it was time to change her life, Lynn embarked on an avid study of spirituality more than a decade ago. These spiritual paths led her to Discover the Gift. In 1999 Lynn completed the Land- mark Forum. After having a life-changing experience during the course, she spent the next four years studying at Landmark, ultimately com- pleting a one-year international leadership training program known as the Introduction Leaders

Program. She then went on to study Kabbalah with Eitan Yardeni and completed the Hoffman Process. Currently Lynn is writing her first children's book, *Brutus*. Being the seeker of knowledge that she is, she continues to study all of the above disciplines, as well as Esther Hicks and the Al-Anon program.

SONIA POWERS, PH.D.

An accomplished lecturer, author, success coach, and transformational speaker, the late Sonia Powers pioneered a series of custom-designed workshops and powerful presentations designed for organizations and companies wishing to achieve a higher level of sustainable quality and productivity.

SIR KEN ROBINSON, PH.D.

Sir Ken Robinson, author of *The Element*, is an internationally recognized leader in the development of creativity, innovation, and human resources. He has worked with governments in Europe, Asia, and the United States and with international agencies, Fortune 500 companies, and some of the world's leading cultural organizations.

RICK ROSS

Rick Ross is a convicted drug trafficker who was brought to national at- tention by a series of articles in the *San Jose Mercury* and the documentary *American Drug War*, both of which highlighted the connection between his case and the Iran-Contra Affair. He now works to bolster at-risk communities while founding a nonprofit organization to help under- privileged youth.

CYNTHIA M. RUIZ, M.S .

Environmentalist, author, and community activist Cynthia M. Ruiz cur- rently serves as the president of the Board of Public Works for the City of Los Angeles. Her experience is diverse and includes teaching, media- tion, civic involvement, and leading workshops.

HIS HOLINESS SRI SRI R AVI SHANKAR

His Holiness Sri Sri Ravi Shankar is a renowned spiritual leader and multifaceted humanitarian whose mission of uniting the world into a violence-free family has inspired millions worldwide. An icon of nonvio- lence and universal human values, he seeks global peace through service and dialogue. He is the founder and spiritual leader of the Art of Living Foundation.

ANDREW SOLIZ

A ceremonialist who serves through traditional Native American cer- emonies, including spirit callings, sweat lodges, and more, Andrew Soliz is also the founder and president of the nonprofit organization Sacred Ways, which works with youth, adults, families, and at-risk populations to promote growth and healing through these teachings and rituals.

CHRISTINE STEVENS, M.S . W.

Christine Stevens is an internationally acclaimed author, music therapist, and speaker. The founder of UpBeat Drum Circles, she is a frequent contributing writer on music and wellness. She has drummed with many Fortune 500 companies and survivors of Hurricane Katrina in New Or- leans and currently visits Iraq with the Ashti Drum (Peace Drum) con- flict resolution program.

TER RY TILLMAN

Terry Tillman lives a life of service: he supports people in their quest for what they want by encouraging spiritual development, provid- ing personal coaching, and facilitating growth. Through his company, 22/7, Tillman conducts seminars, speaking to groups of fifty to fifteen thousand worldwide. He produces, designs, and facilitates leadership training for organizations and individuals, and coaches executives of all nationalities.

JOE VITALE, PH.D.

Joe Vitale is the founder and president of Hypnotic Marketing Inc. and has also written many books, including the only business book based on the success principles of P. T. Barnum (*There's a Customer Born Every Minute*) and *The American Marketing Association Complete Guide to Small Business Advertising*.

DAVID "AVOCADO" WOLFE, M.S.

With a master's degree in nutrition and a background in science and mechanical engineering, David "Avocado" Wolfe is considered one of the world's top authorities on natural health, beauty nutrition, herbalism, organic superfoods . . . and chocolate.

Shajen Joy Aziz, MEd., MA

Bio

- -

Shajen Joy Aziz holds master's degrees in both psychology and education. She is first author and co-Creator of the international bestselling book and film **Discover the Gift**, which has been released in 22 countries worldwide. A founding member of the Association of Transformational Leaders, Shajen Joy is an acclaimed speaker and educator with an extensive web presence and a devoted fan base. Her work has been featured in The Huffington Post, CNN, ABC, NBC, Spirit and Destiny Magazine, Examiner.com, Spiritual Networks, Life Connections, Vision Magazine, among many others.

Shajen's work focuses on emotions and systems and their impact on an individuals' ability to thrive personally, professionally, psychologically, and spiritually. She owes her deep understanding of humans and how to improve systems to her twenty years of experience as a Public School Administrator, School Counselor, Program Creator/Director, and Special Educator, as well as to her family and all the students, teachers, parents, clients and systems she has had the pleasure of serving over the years. Shajen holds a Master's Degree in Education from Norwich University and a 2nd Master's Degree in Psychology. She is most passionate about children and young adults, as they are our future. Her motto is "Learning for Life – Empowering the Future".

She brings her years of expertise in education, mental health and human relations to the global movement that is **Discover The Gift**, and is thrilled to be an active force in creating a better world for our children and ourselves.

Shajen has shared the stage with other global Thought Leaders such as Jack Canfield, Sir Ken Robinson, Janet Bray Attwood and Chris Attwood, Rev. Michael Bernard Beckwith, Dr. Barbara De Angelis, David Avocado Wolfe, Rev. Sheila McKeithen, and many more.

"DISCOVER THE GIFT is my passion and purpose as it creates possibilities in our lives and especially in the lives of our children. This work has a global impact as well as a personal one: on you, on your families, your communities, and on the next generation. ... Let's all discover our Gifts and share them with the world. The world is waiting! Everyone is waiting. I'm really excited to see what we have to offer."

~ Shajen Joy Aziz

DEMIAN LICHTENSTEIN
Co-creator

- -

Demian lives in California with his wife, Brooke and their two sons, Romeo and Luke.

Demian Lichtenstein is the coauthor, producer, and director of *Discover the Gift* and a globally recognized transformational leader. He has also di-rected major studio films such as *3000 Miles to Graceland* and music videos for Grammy-winning artists such as Sting and Eric Clapton. He currently serves on the Leadership Council of the Directors Guild of America and is the CEO of Equilibrium Entertainment, where he overseas all creative affairs, worldwide production, financing, and distribution.

Printed in the United States
By Bookmasters